LIVING WITH LIMITS

Theological Musings
For The Twenty-first Century

Harold C. Warlick, Jr.

CSS Publishing Company, Inc., Lima, Ohio

LIVING WITH LIMITS

Library of Congress Cataloging-in-Publication Data

Warlick, Harold C.
    Living with limits : theological musings for the 21st century / Harold C. Warlick, Jr.
        p.   cm.
    ISBN 0-7880-0845-5 (pbk.)
    1. Theology — 20th century. 2. Theology — Forecasting. I. Title.
BT28.W34   1996
230'.044—dc20
                                                                        96-10699
                                                                        CIP

ISBN 0-7880-0845-5   PRINTED IN U.S.A.

Dedicated to the
Breakfast Club,
a meaningful pit-stop
for many along life's
relentless journey.

Table Of Contents

Author's Preface

This work is the outcome of more than thirty years of mental struggle. I have tried to express forthrightly some theological conclusions I have reached on the most important questions I have faced relative to our future as a society in the Western world. Always as I write I try to keep in mind the techniques of two of my mentors, John Killinger and Will Willimon. John, my foremost teacher of written expression, has, since my student days at Vanderbilt, been a gentle yet forceful encourager. Will, whose thoughts and sermons from the pulpit of Duke Chapel often find their themes running throughout my own writing, kindly offers me his limited time and his significant pulpit to express new ideas.

The title and focus for this work were originally prepared for the St. Mary's Episcopal Church Forum, High Point, North Carolina. This eclectic yet dedicated group of laypersons has for six years given critique, commentary, and support to a variety of contemporary topics, many of which have found their way between these covers.

Most of the chapters in this work grew out of sermons preached in the Chas. E. Hayworth Sr. Memorial Chapel. Hundreds of students who have taken Religion 119, Christian Worship, in High Point University, have written papers reflecting on some of these sermons. They have been both a vital source of understanding and an irresistible challenge.

The piece "Being Tested" was originally prepared for the Bishop's Convocation of Clergy of the Western North Carolina Conference of the United Methodist Church. "Shepherds, Strangers, And Aliens" was prepared first for the Thanksgiving Service in Memorial Church, Harvard University, 1993. The pieces on illusion and reality owe a debt to the World Arts and Cultures program at U.C.L.A. and Dean Robert L. Blocker, whose kind invitation to teach there hastened the process of putting random thoughts into finished lectures.

Some of the personal articulations about limits and their potential for self-understanding were given focus by Dr. Dennis Kennedy of Winston-Salem, North Carolina, and by my wife, Diane Norman Warlick, who has turned the great limitation of having to live with me for 25 years into a creative and loving process.

Finally, this marks twenty years of pleasant association with CSS Publishing Company in general and Wesley Runk and Ellen Shockey in particular. These voices over the telephone, whose faces I have not seen, have been consistently hopeful and helpful in all kinds of weather. My hope is that the book may help readers find a kind of stability in their personal lives similar to the professional stability this fine company has afforded me.

Foreword

The work before you is an effort to provide some theological undergirding for the passing of our Protestant era. Yet it is not a eulogy for the world of the Twentieth Century as known and expressed by mainline Christians. The changes which vex the inherited mainline Judeo-Christian landscape are well known. Many books now include "post-Protestant era" in their subtitles. Elaborate wakes have never amused or intrigued me. I have been more interested in new beginnings and how venerable Christian truths might undergird or contribute to the courage it takes to encounter new experiences.

My efforts to find theological rationale to undergird the Christian life in the modern world were motivated as much by an interest in my own sanity as by an effort to be academically profound. Above all, this book is about growth and change. It reflects a personal journey in, hopefully, comprehendible language.

I am a professor in a university but I also serve as the Minister to the University. I teach and I preach — perhaps poorly but never infrequently. Consequently, my job description represents the schizophrenic lifestyle which seems to confront all Americans as we move toward the twenty-first century. I am caught between the old values and the new realities. I must preach biblical sermons to the same students to whom I try to teach the latest in research and academic principles. I am a white, male Protestant who tries to use inclusive language and open the door to employment opportunities for non-white, non-male individuals who have been too long without being considered for positions like the one I hold. I am a Methodist who preaches each week to a congregation whose largest composition is Roman Catholic. I am now fully in middle

9

age, reflecting on younger days and works I authored about subjects more nailed down than the subject tackled herein. And, like most, I am caught between the inherited Protestant ethic which emphasized hard work, thrift, saving, moderation, and equality of means and the contemporary ethic which emphasizes debt accumulation, hedonism, spending, leisure, and equality of ends. I am caught between the excesses of the past and the limits of the future.

My only hope is that the theological and personal resources I have summoned in these pages to help me make sense of how my life can respond to the current world will help you to think about yourself, your society, and your faith.

Chapter One

Living With Limits

One of the leaders in the world of pastoral psychology is Wayne Oates. When he was a young graduate student, Wayne pastored a small church in Kentucky. He and his wife would commute to the church on Saturdays, hold services on Sundays, and return to the school Sunday evening. On one such occasion they were staying with an old farmer and his wife. After an early dinner, the old farmer and his wife washed the dishes. Then the farmer looked at the young pastor. "Brother Oates," he said, "are you or Mrs. Oates sick?" Wayne responded, "Why, no, we're fine."

"Good," said the farmer. "If you was, me and the missus would sit up with you. Being how you ain't, we'll be going to bed." As the old couple started up the stairs, the farmer turned and said, "Make yourselves at home. You're welcome to anything we have. If there's anything you want and can't find, come up and wake us up. And *we'll come down and teach you how to get along without it.*"[1]

As I look back on life and think about some things I could have learned from my experiences, my education, and my marriage, I believe I would have been well served to have learned how to live more with less.

One of the pivotal features in the Bible is the man called Moses. A lot went right in Moses' life: he was raised by royalty; he was the liberator of his people from slavery; he was the person chosen by God to form his people into a nation and give them the law (the ten commandments). What a stark contrast to those accomplishments is presented to us in the story of the end of Moses' life! Moses is held back from entering the promised land.

He gets to the door, but he doesn't get to go over the threshold with his people. Is this a story of unfulfillment or what? The Bible doesn't really explain this last scene in Moses' life. It doesn't tell us exactly why Moses' life ended within sight of, but not having realized, his life's goals. In fact, we are told that he was buried in a hidden grave. There his remains rest today — unremembered, unmarked, and unknown. Sigmund Freud goes so far as to suggest in *Moses and Monotheism* that Moses, indeed, may have been murdered by his own people.

My friend, Will Willimon,[2] says that the story of Moses goes against our faith in progress, the idea that there is some achievable future which we can control. In short, we tend to like stories with happy endings. Do this, do that, control your life and you'll live happily ever after. Yet, in reality, a good deal of life is spent just on the verge of the threshold but not over it. There is much incompleteness in this life and we, like Moses, must come to terms with that incompleteness.

I am slowly learning that the most important virtue in life is *patience*. Now, this comes to you from one who for most of his life had no patience at all. Part of that eventuates from my misinterpretation of my father, who had the patience of Job. When he was cutting the lawn my father would stop the mower and move the grasshoppers to the side to keep from running over them. Determined to pass him in career and economic affluence, I regarded his patience as a liability instead of an asset. I was going to make things happen and control my future. And so many things worked out well for me that I was unintentionally deluded into thinking that it is possible to plan and organize your life in such a way that all things work out well. There must be a reason behind everything and so we press and work and get angry when things don't work out well. Right?

Well, that is apparently not life. One of the fortunate aspects of life for our generation may be the current shrinking economic picture in America and the necessity for both women and men to work hard and be aware of limits. You see, rather than something we can always control, life is an accumulation of decisions that could have been made differently, things that often didn't work as planned, and words that came out wrong.

The chief issue for us may be how to learn to live with these limits and how to live *more* in the face of them. The great theologian Paul Tillich once contended that the goal of life is for us humans to live up to our potential without trying to live beyond our limitations. Perhaps a fitting place to begin is with this experience we call "marriage."

Marriage is not "finding the right person." Even if we find the right person at age 23 or 24, we will find the very next year that that person has changed. And, so will *we* have changed. That's why in marriage ceremonies we are not asked if we are certain we have the right person. All we are asked is our willingness to risk with this person, even in moments when this person is not right, for better or worse, richer or poorer, sicker or healthier. The willingness to risk through life's successes and *regrets* is the key. To learn to be patient and come to terms with the incompleteness in our lives, of course, takes both partners, and real courage.

Most of us are going to work, train, retrain, do continuing education, and be away from our spouse and children much more than was the case in previous generations. This will put some pressure on our time together with the significant people in our lives. Again we will have to learn to live more with less. I worry about people who have to process conversations for endless hours on end, talking until 5 a.m. to get to something significant. It shows a lack of trust and acceptance of incompleteness.

I agree with Anna Quindlen of the *New York Times*[3] that our impatient and untrusting world has created a horrible concept called *quality* time. Quality time. That concept puts a lot of pressure on people. Here is someone going around living a fairly uneventful and humdrum evening and in comes this beacon of light ready for a good time to be had by all. "I took the whole afternoon off to be here and all you're doing is bickering."

One of the biggest disadvantages looming in our future will be the paucity of hours we will have to spend with our loved ones. It could make us horribly committed to quality time.

Every moment does not have to count. Real life is sometimes just sitting across the room from another person reading. Real life is sometimes bickering. Real life is sometimes staring off into the distance. Real life is often what happens between the exciting excursions. We must learn how to make peace with that.

An old parable[4] sums it up pretty well. Three persons who were down on their luck were sitting around a campfire talking. One of them said, "I used to live in a fine house and drive a Mercedes; then the economy failed and I lost everything. God is to blame for my troubles. My family's expectations are to blame for my troubles." The second person, a woman, said, "I had a sauna and owned horses. The same thing happened to me. I dislike God and my family as much as you do."

The third person took a long drink of coffee from the tin cup he was holding and looked thoughtful. "I too was a wealthy man," he said, "though I didn't know it at the time. But now I have a new perspective on life. Where I once spent my energy acquiring things, I now spend it enjoying things. Praise God, this is a wonderful cup of coffee! Wouldn't you like some of it?"

Being Tested

The temptation to measure life in terms of consumer acquisition is forcing Americans into a most unhealthy assessment of life. Sometimes societies reach a crossroad. We contemporary Americans are like poor "Chippie," the parakeet.[5]

It all began for Chippie when his owner decided to save time by cleaning his cage with the vacuum cleaner. She removed the attachment from the hose and stuck the hose in the bottom of his cage. At that moment the telephone rang. As she turned to answer it, she lost her aim. As she said "Hello" she heard — "sssoooppp!" Chippie had been sucked into the vacuum cleaner.

Quickly she turned off the vacuum cleaner and opened the bag. The bird was still alive but badly stunned. Chippie was covered with dirt and soot. He resembled a grey ball with two little eyes and a beak protruding from it. In panic she ran to the bathroom sink and turned on the faucet. She held Chippie under the running water for a few minutes. This cleaned the poor bird but left him soaked and shivering. Consequently, she did what any compassionate and quick thinking person would do — she grabbed the hair dryer and blasted Chippie dry with hot air.

14

A few days later the local newspaper writer who had initially reported the incident called Chippie's owner. "Has the bird recovered?" he asked. "Well," the woman replied, "he looks the same. But Chippie doesn't sing anymore. He just sorta' sits and stares." No wonder. Sucked in, washed out, and blown dry. That would steal the voice from any of us.

Many of the younger adults in our world look toward the future and it seems that they are not singing anymore. I think it has to do with more than just an uncertain economic future. Most of us don't know why we aren't singing anymore. *Having been sucked in by the excesses of the 1950s and 1960s, washed off by the "me generation" of the 1970s and 1980s, and blown dry by the shallow, spiritual hot air of the 1990s, we are perhaps being tested in ways we have never before been tested.*

Now, testing is nothing new for this generation. In fact, today's Americans are perhaps the most tested human beings in the world. We've even coined a new psychological and educational phrase: "He's real smart; he just doesn't test well." And if little Johnny does make it past the CAT, ACT, SAT, and other tests, chances are he'll have to take a polygraph test in his interview to get a job and take random drug tests to keep his job. Over fifty percent of the Fortune 500 companies use drug tests as a way of assessing employee capabilities.

Being tested or tempted, of course, is nothing new for one's religious life. Jesus Christ told a parable of two house builders. One built his house on sand and the other on rock. When the turbulent waters came and tested the house, the house built on a foundation of sand was washed away.

As I reread the tests or temptations of Jesus in the wilderness, one thing keeps jumping out at me. Satan kept throwing before Jesus *excessive expectations.* Satan kept running back into the past and quoting *abnormal* scriptural references as if Jesus would take the bait and consider it something He should expect to be *normal.* The tempter said, "If you are really the Son of God, then you will be able to turn stones into bread." But Jesus kept shifting the emphasis away from these excessive promises. Finally, Satan offered Him all the kingdoms of the world. In fact, he offered

Him things Satan had no ability to deliver. It was an impossible dream. Jesus kept things in proportion: He knew his history; He knew scripture; He knew that He would not face imminent ruin if these things were not handed to Him not only at the start of His ministry, but even in His lifetime. He did not get sucked in, washed off and blown dry by excessive promises. *He refused to let abnormal promises become His norm for living.*

Apparently, Jesus was consistent in this. One day He took Peter, James, and John up to a high mountain. There Jesus' clothes became white as light and His face shone like the sun. Just then Moses and Elijah appeared, talking with Jesus. Peter was excited. "Let's build three shelters and stay here," Peter implored. But Jesus led them down and said, "Tell no one about this." Again, Jesus did not want the *abnormal* to become a *normal* expectation.

I tell you this because I believe that we must not fail this same test. We have never developed an ideal of contentment in America because of our *abnormal* quest for more. We find ourselves with a real test today because our reference point of normalcy was never normal in the first place. A lot of people are upset about our economy, the job market, religion, and the American dream and say "Once things get back to normal, once we get the right people hired or elected, or once we get the economy heated up, everything will return to *normal*." But let's take a careful look at our idea of *normal*. Was it really normal?

The median age in the United States currently stands at roughly 36 years. This means that the typical American was born in the late 1950s. The fifties have become our reference point for what's normal.

Let's look carefully at getting back to the normal situation of the gospel of growth in the 1950s and 1960s. Laurence Shamus in his book *The Hunger for More*[6] makes some interesting points.

Was it normal that, after 200 years of worldwide decline in the birthrate of industrialized nations, Americans should go on a binge that made marriage and children almost universal? The population of our country increased by fifty percent between 1946 and 1964. Was that normal? Other western nations returned to pre-war levels of reproduction.

Virtually every church was full 1946-64. Church buildings passed 1 billion dollars in indebtedness. Youth programs were burgeoning. The Boy and Girl Scouts were packing them in like sardines. All colleges were popping at the seams. Was that normal? If we just get the right youth director, the right preacher, the right teachers, the right deans and presidents, is *normal* going to come back?

Was it normal that a nation with seven percent of the world's people should produce two-thirds of its manufactured products, own three-fourths of its cars and appliances, and purchase 33 percent of all the goods available on earth, as the United States did in the 1950s? Can we heat up and get back to normal?

Was it normal that the operating budget of General Motors was larger than that of Poland, or that Americans spent more on going to movies than it cost to run Switzerland? Was that normal?

Was it *normal* that the average American should eat three and a half times as much food as the average foreigner or that his income should be fifteen times as great? Was that normal?

Was it *normal* that by 1964, for the first time in the history of the world, one nation's citizens, ours, were able to pay for the necessities of food, clothing and shelter with less than *half* their after-tax income? Was that normal?

None of these things were normal. They were giddily abnormal. It wasn't that we were competing more successfully those years. There was no competition. With no bombed factories and an undiluted dollar, America stood alone. And this was not *normal*.

You say, well, it seemed normal. Contextual values always seem normal. A bug that lives in a jar of horseradish thinks a horseradish world is normal. During the nineteenth century British Empire every local from London to Bombay surely aspired to sip Earl Grey tea, put jelly on meat and learn to play squash. Such views, of course, are flattering. But when *abnormal* becomes normal a big crossroads is reached when parity is reestablished. When you do get back to normal, that seems like an abnormal defeat, even a humiliation.

There are parents in this world who are wringing their hands over little Johnny or little Susie. Why aren't they normal? Why can't she get a good job like I had at her age? What's wrong with him? He isn't normal. Twenty-six years old and still living at home. "Why, when I was his age I ... My God, it's awful. We're falling apart."

To be certain, in 1959, a thirty-year-old could look forward to a gain of 49 percent in real earnings by his or her fortieth birthday. The Reagan years notwithstanding, in the 1980s real earnings declined an annual average of .3 percent. What's wrong with Johnny? Nothing. He's normal.

The middle-aged person looks back over life and says, "If I had my life to do over I'd do it different. I didn't have this freedom or that freedom. My needs aren't being met. I'm out of this family. Let me out of this marriage." Too bad. Actually, the dream was never normal. Why, if you took the Barbie doll and expanded her to human measurements she would have been 39-23-33. Is that normal? Even if they went back to 1965 and did it differently, I doubt that those people would be any more content today if they still followed that old abnormal dream. Second marriages have a higher divorce rate than first marriages.

And therapists don't help us much by only helping people get in touch with their past. First, we've got to realize that everyone's past was abnormal and everyone's expectations were not normal.

So how do we pass the test? I'm no prophet, but I think with Jesus we can say, "Get behind me Satan, don't try to normalize excessive quotes from the past."

We should feel good about ourselves and our world. We've got a normally bright future, as bright as anyone's has *normally* been in our world. Don't put the pressure on yourself to feel like a failure just because you live in a normal world. This country is not running out of wealth. The American worker is not lazy. We are not running out of drive or facing imminent ruin. We *are* running out of abnormality.

Suicide is now the third leading killer among adolescents. In many cases the real killer is the fact that people felt like failures when all they were was normal. Don't let this world squeeze you into its mold. All you are asked to be is normal.

For generations, people have tried to pass their parents as a genuine sign of contentment. Let me tell you how we can pass our parents' generation and make a genuine contribution to American life.

Our values are essentially the same as our parents. In 1964, the number one value as espoused in random values testing in America was "family security," taking care of your loved ones. That same value was number one in 1971 and 1984. A psychologist, Alberta Herron, and I surveyed a class of university students. Number one value: family security. If we can stand at this cross-roads in American history and refuse to get sucked up, washed off, and blown dry by the past, our divorce rate will not be as high as our parents' generation. We have too many people so driven toward affluence and success that it has cost them their marriages, their families, and their physical health. If we can pass the test and refuse to let the abnormal experiences of the '50s become our *norm* for living, we can perhaps pass our parents' generation in *contentment*. Measuring *more* is easy; measuring *better* is hard. Even in sex, especially we men know how to measure more times instead of better. The way we treat our women is like going through the quality of hamburger meat at a grocery store instead of respecting their personhood. I don't hold myself aloof; I'm part of this generation, too.

The younger generation can pass the previous generation in church life, too, maybe not in numbers but in quality. My generation wants entertainment. My generation doesn't demand much intelligent preaching these days. You can close your eyes and sometimes in church you can't tell where "Dear Abby" stops and Jesus' concern for the world begins. My generation throws pizza parties, retreats, ski trips, lock-ins, and money at our children. Perhaps at some point, due to our limitations, we will encourage substance and not worry about numbers and entertainment as much as we do wisdom.

If we are to acquire some genuine wisdom in living with limits, we must reconnect with some ancient ethical precepts to focus our efforts at community in a pluralistic world. The abnormal America of the 1950s and 1960s was essentially a society of Protestant, Catholic, and Jew. Even the most casual observer of the American scene recognizes the increased impact world religions and Eastern philosophies have made on our society. This impact has reached the most entrenched and traditional institutions in our land. Not only are ethnic churches our fastest growing, but currently Asian-Americans account for twenty percent of the freshman class at Harvard. Certainly the American of today must live with the reality of his or her ethnic origin (both whites and/or blacks) being a more limited slice of the pie of national origin in America. Yet our Judeo-Christian heritage appears to be an exclusive Western religion wrapped around sacred writings that emphasize agricultural motifs. Can we find relevance for today's pluralistic world amid the Biblical symbolism of shepherds, sheep, goats, aliens, and strangers?

Shepherds, Strangers, And Aliens

The major religious obligation upon the Israel of the Old Testament was to take responsibility for the welfare of three powerless groups of people: widows, orphans, and foreigners. Whatever shepherding function Israel had as a nation and whatever role her priests were to play as shepherds of Yahweh's flock, the Torah and the Bible generally emphasized the duty to treat foreigners as fairly as one is commanded to treat a citizen. The *stranger*, in the biblical ethos, referred to foreign residents. Drawing impetus from her own sojourn in Egypt, Israel was expected to empathize with the alien. The levitical law required a special type of welfare for the poor and the immigrant. It was the practice in ancient Israel to cut the stalks of grain with one hand while catching what was reaped with the other hand. Whatever the reaper failed to catch fell to the ground. This was to be left ungathered for the poor and the immigrant, the foreigner. In similar fashion, one could not pick a vineyard bare or gather all the fallen fruit. Only the poor and the stranger could gather or pick certain fruit from the vineyards.[7]

With the priests as the figurative shepherds of the nation such was an effective policy of welfare and a more than adequate response to *immigration*.

20

Ah, but things seldom stay as they are intended. Even shepherds and priests become affluent and allow subtle changes in perception which promote taking care of one's own kind to the exclusion of assisting foreigners or aliens. The word "stranger" has a sad history in the Judeo-Christian perspective. Originally "stranger" described a person without possessions living in another country, but expected to be accorded the privileges of a citizen. As society became more affluent and supposedly more educated, "stranger" came to mean a person "perverse in his or her ways," "a barbarian," an "adulteress," or "not of one's own household." The height of embarrassment came when "stranger" came to mean a convert to Judaism.

An incessant preoccupation with self has for 4,000 years been the curse of religions, the curse of nations, the curse of churches, the curse of individuals, and even the curse of universities. Our notion of a stranger is far removed from the origin of the term as an alien.

We shepherds of academe and church can fall prey to the subtle shift in meaning from alien to stranger. As academicians and preachers, we pride ourselves on our openness to women and blacks. We have taken in those former strangers to our professions. Or have we? In some ways we have merely been willing to embrace women and minorities who have adopted the goals, ambitions, and cultural perspectives of white males. If they think and act as we expect, then, "Welcome, stranger." But if they remain *alien* in their attitudes, their cultural assumptions and their goals, sometimes they find that they are not so welcomed.

One of the key ethical dilemmas is *the argument for an obligation to assist strangers* as over and against *the argument for taking care of our own kind*. This dilemma is the heart of Jesus' parable about the last judgment. From Israel's early existence she not only felt she had sufficient grain and grapes to reduce poverty, but she viewed taking care of the alien as literally taking care of her own. The alien was to be treated as one of her citizens and accorded all the rights of the same.

But as time passed, arguments became pitted against one another, as ultimately they do in all complex societies. If we truly take care of our own, will we have enough resources to assist these homeless strangers? If we feel an obligation to assist the stranger, in everything from welfare to foreign aid, will we be able to care adequately for our own?

Historically such arguments usually lead to a horrible process of transferred resentments. Not only do we have sheep and goats in our world, but quite often morally bankrupt shepherds try to reinforce our perception that those we view as goats are to blame for society's problems.

From a perspective of welcoming the alien or the foreigner, ancient Israel, under the leadership of bad shepherds, began to view her sexual problems, her economic instability, and her political crises as the *result* of having welcomed the stranger. Most of her resentments were transferred to those who were foreign to her ethos. It's human nature for individuals and societies to create images that divert, justify, and transfer our personal fears to others.

I'm ashamed to say that in my own life at the personal level the process of transference for many years went something like this: A church member would come by the church office and complain, nag, and criticize. I would soothingly melt the conflict with the sweet syrup of apology. After all, in a volunteer institution one disgruntled parishioner can create much trouble. Then I would go home and with only minor, if any, provocation, yell at my wife. Many of the statements I would yell should have been heaped on the head of the church member. Often my wife would yell at our oldest son, Scott. He would then pick a fight with our younger son. The younger son had no one weaker than he to lash out at so he would go crying into the yard. There he would pick up a stick and throw it at the dog, a black Lab named Deacon. Well, twice a week ole Deacon got her turn. She would lie in wait for the garbage truck. When she heard it turn the corner she would go berserk. With her ruff up, her eyes wild, and all the fanfare you can imagine, she would snarl and bark like a deranged animal. She would make a wild, self-righteous dash down the driveway like she was going to commit assault and battery on the truck to protect our home.

Here would be these two people, just doing their job, unaware that they were the objects of all our transferred resentments.

We higher animals create images that justify a transfer of the ethical obligation to assist into a self-righteous view of protecting our own kind. We create scapegoats to bear our own sins away. The Germans had the Jews to blame for their problems; the white Southerner had the Negro; the American patriot had the Communists; the Jews and Christians had the Muslims; the male had the female; and now some people have white males.

The hottest issues being currently debated in our country deal with the obligation to assist others versus taking care of our own kind. Shepherds, strangers, and foreigners! Can we create a health care system that will be able to give those who have been powerless, foreign, and strange to its resources the right to be treated as full citizens? Can the North American Free Trade Agreement focus on the issues of trade, environment, health, hunger and human rights in the border counties of Mexico where forty percent of the population lives in poverty? And will the nation of Israel and the PLO be able to find some religious support for treating one another as citizens?

No other piece of Jesus' recorded teaching expresses so eloquently and beautifully the original ethical spirit of the Old Testament and Judaism as his parable of the Last Judgment (Matthew 25). The most striking note of the parable is that many, though they have not known it, have been on God's side all the time. And those who think themselves sheep and on God's side actually are the ones most separated from God. In a rather ironic way, it turns out that the self-righteous who have followed ignorant professors, blind guides, and morally corrupt shepherds, have in their refusal to care for the powerless stranger, refused to care for Jesus himself.

The parable of the Last Judgment clearly states that all the nations of the earth are gathered before Jesus. It is true, after all, that *morals touch everyone*. Briefly stated, this is why ethics courses are almost always required by colleges and universities. Colleges and universities produce our society's *shepherds*. And private universities like ours produce the majority of those shepherds: lawyers, doctors, teachers, ministers, and CEO's of companies.

23

These shepherds are united by one common ethical dilemma. Jesus is correct. Whether in science, economics, government, education, medicine or religion, the last ethical judgment always revolves around the proper utilization and distribution of one's limited resources, including the years of one's life: the obligation to assist the powerless stranger or the obligation to conscript those same resources in the act of taking care of one's own kind.

Obviously the key to accepting the morality of a pluralistic world is to examine our perception of power and authority. One of the most critical limits we face in life is the limitation of our *human* power. Human power and human authority are, indeed, quite limited.

Power And Authority

In some ways human beings seem to have changed little through the centuries. When we humans are threatened by someone or we find ourselves unwilling to accept what someone is saying to us, we try to discredit him. And the first line of attack is always the same: we question credentials. S/he is not properly approved or certified. S/he doesn't have the right authority to be a part of us.

Now, rather amazingly, this has been the tactic since the beginning. If you read the Bible carefully you will find that the chief priests and scribes never denied that Jesus performed miracles. They never denied He was a powerful preacher and teacher. No one even claimed He was a fake, that He did not really walk on water or turn water into wine. But each of the Gospels records that the chief priests and scribes questioned the *authority* of Jesus, His credentials. Few, if any, questioned the truth of what He said. They just took issue with His claims to authority. He had not been properly *certified.* He did not have the kind of pedigree or authority some people thought a son of God should have.

This Jesus did not have the credentials to do what He was doing. He was not the kind of person those who considered themselves in the know wanted to associate with.

He came from the ranks of the poor and the uneducated, first of all. Therefore He had no authority with the power brokers of

24

Israel. His earthly parent, Joseph, was a common carpenter. Jesus' tastes, His dress and His primary interests were rooted in the needs and concerns of poor people. His vocabulary was limited. He worked with His hands. In addition, His disciples were ordinary people without fancy titles or prestige. So the chief complaint of the Pharisees and Sadducees was "He just isn't our type."

How prevailing is that charge. I remember sitting in my residence hall one night my senior year in college when the Greeks were giving out their bids. I was the Resident Advisor. When several of my sophomore friends returned to their room, they had rather exhausted looks on their faces. I knew they liked a boy named Pete. "Well," I asked, "did you guys take ole Pete in?" They rather sheepishly replied, "No."

"No!" I retorted. "Why not? Did he not have the grades? Did he pick his nose or belch at the wrong time? Did he lie, cheat, steal, or get drunk?"

They responded: "You know, Hal, he's just not our type. He's not the kind of person who would fit well in our group." In other words, they were telling me Pete didn't have the kind of credentials they wanted.

For all that we preach against totalitarian authority over us, our very pattern of life is based upon recognition of authority and examination of credentials. And it is a most difficult problem trying to live in a pluralistic world with individuals who do not possess the credentials we habitually value.

We behave as if we were people of great authority. As Bertrand Russell has said, we carry with us a swarm of comfortable credentials which follow us like flies on a hot day. We are a "chosen people"; we are a superior racial minority; we are invincible Americans in war and wealth; we believe in the worthwhileness of our businesses. Give us security, status, and safety and we will make sure life turns out right!

Then at some point in every life comes the kicker which reminds us of how powerless we really are even in the midst of the right kind of people who fit so well in our groups. Cancer, poor health, wild children, wars, accidents, credit, debts, suits, courts, ah, but they do come to us, these threats to our human authority. If we

25

live long enough we find that the true axiom is not "every dog has his day" but *every day has its dog*!

Our human powers reach their limits. So with all our degrees hanging on the walls of our den, the expensive cars parked in the garage of the big house in the nice neighborhood, and the calendar filled with important meetings with important people in important places, we combat the loss of power as best we can. Pepto-Bismol and Maalox slow down our stomach juices and hydrochloric acid speeds them up. Aspirin can provide a minor insulation and Demorol, a blackout. And as Carlyle Marney said: "Beer will break the ice, and vodka will melt it."[8] All these things help insulate us from the fact that human power can go just so far. Hear me out because *I am talking about our future.*

Ultimately all *human* powers and all *human* authorities end. The Gospel of Matthew brings us to a scene that illustrates the authority of humans as over against the authority of Jesus. Jesus enters a small town named Capernaum. As He is walking along He is met by a centurion who desperately needs His help.

The centurion represented the ultimate in human authority. Such a person commanded a hundred men in the Roman army. He had the authority to give orders. When he issued an order a soldier was expected to obey it without question. Behind the authority granted the centurion was the authority of his leaders, and behind them was the authority of Caesar. There was no greater earthly authority in terms of the power of warfare and government.

Yet the centurion knew his power was limited and his authority was different from the authority of Jesus. The centurion had authority over soldiers. Jesus has authority over life itself. The centurion's problems could not be solved by human power or human authority. He approached Jesus in behalf of his servant who was ill. His rank and power fell away as he replied, "Lord, I am not worthy that you should even come under my roof."

What we have here are two radically different types of authority, as different as day from night. There are different purposes and larger interests than those affected by the credentials you and I fight so hard to obtain.

We do not create ourselves and we do not have the power of judgment which sets a final bound to the evil in our world. The mystery of life lies in the fact that the weakness of love is the ultimate power in life and authority over life. The Christ upon the cross rises above all philosophies and securities humans can construct. This weakness of God, this pouring out all in love, is the final power and the ultimate authority of God.

How utterly insignificant some people look to us in terms of their credentials and their power. From a human point of view most true political, educational, and religious power appears puny and weak. Don't be fooled by this. The greatest achievement in the history of education was made by a woman born unable to see, unable to speak, and unable to hear. In music, the greatest symphonies were written by a composer who was stone deaf.

The man who molded his nation's public opinion into a force so invincible it toppled the British Empire was a toothless, spindly-legged, oriental mystic, who wandered from place to place in a loincloth.[9]

Perhaps the most significant discovery in history, the law of gravity, was made by a person so cruelly lampooned that his critics called him a deranged poet.

As we cast backward glances at the Helen Kellers, Beethovens, Gandhis, Isaac Newtons and Jesus Christs of our human history, the juxtapositions of powers and authorities are quite clear. Human power is limited. All human authority is temporary. Only that which has created us and is the ultimate judge of the evil in the world has ultimate power and authority over life.

The most critical question we can ask ourselves is this one: By what authority is my life to be governed? Human or divine?

If we are to acknowledge the limits of our own power and authority, then, obviously, finding a place to hide with members of our own kind becomes futile. Ultimately there is nowhere to hide from an authority and power that lie beyond our human existence. This limitation may be our source of salvation as well as our inspiration for creating and sustaining community in a world that is equally limited.

Nowhere To Hide

I don't like to be evaluated. Consequently, I find it very difficult to evaluate others. Grades are often as big a problem to professors as they are to students. It's not easy to give a *B, C, D,* or *F.* Giving an *A* or receiving an *A* is easy. Everyone likes an *A.* But those grades below that tend to make us uneasy. They remind us that we are vulnerable, something less than perfect. And often they create anxiety as we try to accept the realities of our lives. Am I that bad a teacher? Is she that bad a student?

I suppose my anxiety over grades began early. When I was five years old my parents sent me to this institution called kindergarten. I was happy. All my friends had been students for a year and it didn't seem fair to me that they got to go to school while I had to stay home by myself. Now I was a student, too. All went well for two months in this thing called school. We played, counted, read, and learned a few things. Then, one Friday, the teacher, Mrs. Gibson, handed to each one of us a large brown envelope. "This is your report card," she said. "Take it home, have your parents sign it, and bring it back Monday."

Report card! What's that? Not daring to open the sealed brown envelope, I approached one of the older kids in the neighborhood, a sixth grader. This guy was wise. "What's a report card?" I asked. "Oh, man," he exclaimed. "You take that thing home to your parents every six weeks and they yell at you, scream at each other, throw things around, and beat the crap out of you."

Well, my anxiety level went through the roof. I felt exposed. What could I do? I had to find a place to hide that envelope. Maybe the teacher would forget she'd given it to me. Late in the afternoon as early evening's shadows crept across the yard, I slithered past the house to the garage. Beside the garage stood the huge garbage can. Quietly but quickly I tossed in that still unopened brown envelope. Then I ran back into the house as fast as I could run. The envelope scared me; I felt naked and vulnerable. I was afraid. So I hid it.

The next day was Saturday. My mother and I were downtown at the department store. As we went through the checkout line, the cashier, a neighbor, proudly proclaimed to my mother, "My Tommy had an excellent report card from Mrs. Gibson. How did Harold, Jr., do on his report card?" I tried to go through the cracks in the floor but they wouldn't swallow me. I tried to edge behind the counter but my mother had grabbed my arm. There was nowhere to hide. Nowhere to hide.

After a wild drive home, I found myself rummaging down in the bottom of the trash can. My mother watched over me like a gestapo agent in hot pursuit. There was nowhere to hide. Finally, I ripped open the envelope and produced the card. It said: "Harold is progressing nicely. He colors especially well and stays between the lines."

That was it! That's all it said. Why had I listened to that slimy serpent of a sixth grader? *I had sought wisdom and wound up vulnerable, afraid, and in hiding.*

I wish that was the only time that has happened in my life, especially when the stakes were much bigger than a kindergarten sealed report.

There's a story in scripture that is as old as any we have that points to a salient fact about us humans. Adam, which means "humankind," and Eve, which means "mother of all living," are in a predicament. They are in hiding. They are trying to outrun God. They are vulnerable. Their lives are controlled by anxiety. They hear the footsteps of God moving around the Garden looking for them. They are aware that they are naked and weak. Once they were happy but now they are wiser. God catches them. After all, who can run from God? Finally humankind answers God: "I tried to get away ... I was afraid ... I was naked ... I ate ... I *hid*."

Believe it or not, the story of Adam and Eve is our story. One of the most prominent and respected persons I have ever heard of just up and quit his job one day. He finally had run out of places to hide. Always he had been a moving target. And his words are somewhat prophetic: "I was so good at what I did everyone thought it came easy for me. But it was so hard. People thought it was easy for me because I was good at it. I just wanted to hide and make it all go away. But there was just nowhere to hide. I would have given anything to be out of the spotlight but there was just nowhere to hide."

At some point in your life you will look composed and self-assured to the outside world. Many will think you wise. But you'll be running scared on the inside, feeling vulnerable, naked, and

29

anxious. Somewhere in the silent shadows it will dawn on you that there is nowhere to hide.

You'll feel unimportant in your family and there'll be nowhere to hide.

You'll try so very hard in vain to please your parents and there'll be nowhere to hide.

You'll know that you really don't want all those things you are working so hard to buy and your loved ones could be happier, much happier, with so much less but there'll be nowhere to hide.

You'll wonder even why people who think you should be excited to be off in college and finally getting away from home can't understand how frightened you are — and there'll be nowhere to hide.

It's a common reality when it hits you — whether out loud, whispered down low, or just thought of inside you. We all fear being "found out" and there's nowhere to hide. At that point we must face our limits or continue to fake it.

The Bible, above all, is a book of reality. The fingerprints of human difficulty are stamped all over it. Most of the Psalms were composed in times of deep anxiety and personal fear. The majority of Paul's letters were authored in prison. There are no knights in shining armor or princesses with golden tiaras among the biblical heroes and heroines. They're just ordinary men and women struggling through the difficulties of life who discover when they've run out of places to hide that there is the grace of God standing there in their silent shadows.

Perhaps the most obvious example in scripture is the man named Peter. He was an outwardly forceful and confident leader. But inwardly he was an anxious man whose response to reality was often to run into the shadows to try to find a place to hide. When he was confronted in the courtyard after Jesus was arrested, a maiden asked him if he had known Jesus. Wasn't he a disciple? "Not me!" he declared. "Girl, I tell you I don't know the man." Then Peter tried to blend in with the crowd and find a place to hide.

And after the resurrection Jesus found Peter and some of the disciples back in their boats out fishing. They were trying to hide and pretend nothing had happened.

30

Still later Peter was eating with some Gentiles at the table, trying to expand his consciousness. But, lo and behold, some of the leading Jewish fundamentalists from Jerusalem came into the room. Know what Peter did? He was so intimidated and anxious that he picked up his plate and moved to a Jewish table. There he tried to hide and blend in with the crowd so nobody would know he'd been eating with different people. Paul got so angry at this that he started cursing Peter and calling him names.

This finding a place to hide with your own kind in a pluralistic and limited world isn't first century material, is it?

The story of Adam and Eve hiding from God is our story, too. God comes to them and clothes them — extends his love to them in their shadowy place of anxiety and fear. But the story unleashes for them and for us a new perspective on life. There are two opposing forces in this ongoing experience called life. One force is constantly building up, looking for us, clothing us, standing there in our vulnerability, nakedness, anxiety, and pain. There is nowhere we can hide from this force called God — no sorrow too big to hide behind, no difficulty too wide to remove us, no pain too great to shield us. That's the good news. The other force, however, is constantly tearing down. Whether it's a slippery serpent or the disorder of a bad decision, this force, too, cannot be escaped ... no success is so large we can hide behind it, and no amount of money or a wonderful spouse can give us a safe hiding place. That's the bad news. We have to choose which force we will join, one that builds us up or one that tears us down.

You would think we would want to join forces with that which is on our side — friends who wish us well and events that make us feel good instead of anxious and afraid when we wake up the next morning. We do have to choose where we will place our energies and our time.

Many good things happen in our lifetimes. There are gentle people and there are ruthless people. We are bombarded by good luck and bad luck, good timing and bad timing. We have a measure of self-worth and peace in our lives and a measure of sex and violence. We may not be able to control what happens to us. But *we are responsible for the degree of attention we choose to give the good or the bad.*

31

This choice is ours, almost like choosing which television channel to watch. We don't choose what comes on and when it is televised but we control what we're going to watch, who we're going to let drive our lives. And that choice is critical. One thing is for certain: there is good and evil in this world and at some point we all realize that *there is nowhere to hide*. We must all face up to our human limitations in the face of a divine power. We cannot hide from God and we cannot hide from ourselves. As we face our limited time on this earth we must learn to limit and control even our memories and our imaginations.

Remember And Forget
One of the fascinating aspects of being human is our ability to create time. We have memories and can literally sit in the present but remember and live in the past. On the other hand we also have imaginations and can literally live in the future. We can imagine what we're going to do as soon as this time of reading is over.

Most of our problems in life don't come from our imaginations. They come from our memories. The past presents us with a paradox. On the one hand, a lot of good things have happened to us. These things, if remembered, can give us great confidence in ourselves each day. Unfortunately, we sometimes forget things we should remember. On the other hand, some bad things have happened to us. We can remember some things we should forget and let them become a lead-weight, dragging us into despair. The prophet Isaiah confronts this two-edged sword in conflicting verses.

At one point he begs his people to remember the former things, those things of long ago. But at another point he is equally adamant in demanding that his people forget the former things and not dwell on the past. Remember and forget. What's happening here? Remember but forget? (Isaiah 46:8; 43:18).

It is a fact that we humans are what we are due to the way we edit and limit our memories. We tend to be selective in terms of what we bring forward from our past.

You know how selective memory works. There are individuals who can memorize and bring forward the exact batting averages to the third decimal point of the entire starting lineup of the Philadelphia Phillies but can't remember a Sunday sermon.

Sometimes entire nations engage in selective memories. Consider the American Revolution. Our national consciousness remembers the determined colonial settler being pitted against the foreign forces of the King of England. Actually Americans fought Americans. Benjamin Franklin stopped speaking to his Tory son. Only a third of the colonists actively supported the war, and we are told by the historians that nearly as many Americans fought *for* Britain as fought *against* Britain.[10]

And consider our wonderful memories of Christopher Columbus. When he arrived in the New World he frequently hanged thirteen Indians at a time in honor of the twelve apostles and Jesus. Every male over fourteen years of age had to bring a quota of gold every three months to the *conquistadors*. Those who could not pay this had their hands cut off "as a lesson." Half the 250,000 Indians on Haiti had been murdered, mutilated or had committed suicide within the first two years following Columbus' discovery of the New World.[11]

Remember and forget. Much of who we are as people and as nations revolves around how we edit and limit our memories. Psychologists assure us that the seeds of so many difficulties we experience in adult life were sown in childhood. Many of our fears, inhibitions, phobias, or what not, come to us out of early childhood experiences which we have not forgotten. We leave our childhood behind and come to adulthood, but those ghosts from the past pursue us.

This is no small matter. How timeless are the truths we find in the Bible about human life. There is an amazing passage of scripture in the account of the Israelites' flight from Egypt. At one point the Angel of God, which went before the Israelites as a cloud, had to go stand behind them to help them close the door on their past. At that juncture it was not so much the threat of the Red Sea in front of the people that created the panic as it was the hosts of Egypt behind them. Harold Cooke Phillips is quite correct: "*Is it not true that often our greatest enemies are not those in front of us but those behind us?*"[12] I know that many of us worry about the job market, the future of our ever-warming planet, and future health threats, from AIDS to cancer. But is it not true that at our base level we, like the Israelites, are harassed not so much by the enemies we must one day meet as by the Egyptians we have already met? This is what makes life so difficult. We have these ghosts pursuing us. We think we have escaped, then we hear the clatter of their horses and see the dust of their chariots! These things harass us because we leave the doors of our memory partly open to them. At some point you and I must set the Lord our God not only before us but behind us — between us and those memories from the past.

In this respect Jesus' words have some healing power. "Love your enemies! Bless those who persecute you. Turn the other cheek. If someone asks you to carry his pack one mile, you carry it two miles." Forgive people, how much, seventy times seven? Why this absurdity? "Parents, don't provoke your children to anger." What is this nonsense? Why?

You make yourself fit for your future as you limit your past. The parents of the Jivaro tribe of Indians in Ecuador have an amazing custom. Every night, when their children go to bed, they linger by their besides. They whisper into the ears of the children the names of all the people they must hate when they are older. This is the tribal way of keeping its feuds alive from generation to generation.

The adults can keep their hatred and negativity alive in the minds of their children. Like an acid in the soul, the constant remembrance of evil can eat away at each generation. Such selected memory is a horrible thing. It creates a lack of emotional confidence in life for each succeeding generation. Very precious things are ruined by keeping old grudges, resentments, and vexations in mind. There are some things we have to forget. If we remember all the hurt we have experienced, life becomes clogged and choked. Life is essentially a process of managing our memories. We should constantly sort out our memories, throwing away things we ought to forget and keeping things that are precious. We either manage our memories or they manage us.

34

This is easy to say and hard to realize. It is not human nature to forget our unpleasant experiences and remember the good. In fact, Ford Motor Company once conducted a survey among its customers. Ford discovered that the people who have had a positive experience with the car they purchase tell an average of two other persons about that good experience. But the customer who has purchased a lemon of an automobile or had a bad experience with the service department tells an average of thirteen other persons. That's the way we humans are: we remember the ugliness and forget the beauty; we hold to the hate and let go of the love; we remember the cruelty rather than the kindness.

One of the amazing tendencies in life is the ability of evil in the world to shake our faith in God. We all worry about the problem of evil. We have courses on Death and Dying and the Theodicy issue which, simply put, means if God is all powerful, all knowing, and all loving, why do good things happen to bad people and bad things to good people?

But isn't the presence of good just as big an issue? If there is no God, how do we explain the good? Where did it come from? Isn't the problem of good as big an issue as the problem of evil? How do we account for the beauty of Beethoven, the compassion of Martin Luther King, or the courage of Joan of Arc? Was Jesus merely an accidental collection of atoms?

Be careful what you remember. There are painful failures in life. There are ghosts from our past that come charging into our present. There are doors that we have to struggle to keep shut. But that is not all life. In each of us there are some happy memories of times when fortune, even if only for a little while, turned in our favor. Those memories are there to give us joy and confidence, almost like secret helpers, if we do not let the ghosts crowd them out.

Memories are in our lives to strengthen us. And the greatest strength and peace we can know is to get in touch with our childhood knowledge of love. This will take some managing. *Some of us need to recast the memories we have of relationships with our father or mother into adult terms.* Some of us have been moving through life feeling unblessed. We go through life, even if those parents are long ago dead, forever seeking mother's approval or father's approval. Memories gallop into the present from the past. We need to limit what we bring forward into current awareness.

One of the greatest powers in life is to have our God move behind us and protect us from those crippling memories. And all of us have them. It is a truly adult and Christian experience to recast your past and maybe see now that a father's love was there but was overshadowed by a misguided life or the demands of survival.

In like manner, how wonderful to realize a mother's love was there but was overshadowed by a misguided life or by the demands of survival. Instead of forever seeking our father's approval or our mother's approval, we may have to put God back there and find the ways in which our parents are truly imperfect and truly human like us. Making peace, whether face-to-face or in the memory of a relationship, gives us tremendous strength. It also grants us the adulthood we desperately need. We can forget and then we can remember. You see, when we make peace with our past in our own minds the strength of our father and mother and the strength of their father and mother become a well-spring in our own lives.[13]

It is only when we learn to live with limits in a world of broken dreams, blind guides, and ignorant professors that we can open ourselves to a meaningful present.

Chapter Two

Dim Visions
And Blind Guides

The societal limits which impinge on our world also affect our personal existence in profound ways. Nowhere is this more critical than in our own dreams and visions.

Dreams and visions are important in life. Every action we take in life was designed by someone. Every piece of clothing, every building, every hymn book, every chair, every light fixture, and every automobile existed first in someone's vision. Someone had to have the idea or the dream to turn out the product. The same holds true for the way we act. As Jesus said, "The eye is the seat of the body." If you cannot dream it, cannot envision it, then you simply cannot do it.

Dreams and visions can also be very crushing. Not all dreams come true. We invent certain images of ourselves, certain pictures of the way life is supposed to be, and then we are somewhat shocked at the way things do not turn out. Just as the dreams and visions of the 1990s provide an inadequate base for living in a pluralistic world, so, too, do some of our individual aspirations place us on the brink of frustration.

Dr. J. Wallace Hamilton, in his book *Horns and Halos in Human Nature*, tells of one of the weirdest auction sales in history. It was held in the city of Washington, D.C. It was an auction of designs, actually patent models of old inventions that did not make it in the marketplace. There were 150,000 designs up for auction. There was an illuminated cat to scare away mice. There was a device to prevent snoring which consisted of a trumpet reaching from the mouth to the ear. One person designed a tube to reach from his

37

mouth to his feet so that his breath would keep his feet warm as he slept. There was an adjustable pulpit which could be raised or lowered. You could hit a button and make the pulpit descend or ascend to illustrate a point dramatically. Obviously, at one time somebody had high hopes for each of those designs which did not make it.[14] Some people died in poverty, having spent all their money trying to sell their dream. One hundred fifty thousand broken dreams! Is there anything sadder?

If we call God the master designer of the universe, then we must view the New Testament as a book of broken dreams. It begins with a massacre of innocent children by King Herod. It is centered in the execution of its hero. And it ends with the martyred saints crying, "How long, O Lord, how long?" In terms of the design of life, the crucifixion of Jesus caused serious questions to be written in the minds of humanity. There on the cross was a man who loved His enemies, a man whose righteousness was greater than the Pharisees, a man who was rich but became poor, a man who gave His robe to those who took His cloak, a man who prayed for those who despitefully used Him.[15] Yet, society crucified Him, executed Him. The question to ask in the presence of this awesome scene is whether such goodness is the design of the universe or forms an exception. Is life designed to be loving, serving, giving, and dying? Does that design work? Does it pay off? Is it rewarding?

If not, then we perhaps should abandon the Christian approach in favor of hedonism or existentialism. These latter approaches champion the futility of human efforts to find meaning in the face of death. For the hedonist the pursuit of pleasure and the avoidance of pain are the highest goods. If we all die meaningless deaths then we had best grab what pleasures are available to us while we can.

The existentialist is correct in asserting that the human being is the only animal that knows it is going to die. This obvious stress and anxiety can champion a meaningless approach to life. Indeed, why have dreams and visions if we all die anyway?

One of my first lectures to freshmen in our university is centered around an exercise to start them thinking about the meaning of existence. After asking them to write down how they envision leaving their stamp of influence on the world, professionally, personally, religiously, and familiarly, I stump and shock them with a request. I ask, "Now, I would like someone to stand and please call out the first and last names of your great-grandparents!" To date, not one student has been able to rise to the occasion. Obviously, one has to examine one's projected impact on life in the face of the fact that most likely our own great-grandchildren will not even know our name, much less our religious affiliation, our vocation, or our philosophy of life.

We perhaps can identify with the men on the road to Emmaus who were walking and talking with each other following the death of Jesus. They told of all that had happened, how this Jesus of Nazareth, mighty in deed and word before God and all the people, had been condemned to death and crucified.

Are there any clearer words of a broken dream than theirs? "But we had hoped he was the one to redeem Israel" (Luke 24:21). Oh, we had hoped He was the one to make it. We had dreamed He would be the one. But it just didn't work out.

All of us have dreams for ourselves and our lives that just do not make it. We come back home on the Emmaus road with our dream broken in our hip pocket, a sure-fire program that fell flat, a preventive that didn't prevent, a solution that did not solve, a panacea that did not pan out. We wail the plaintive cry, "But we had hoped this would redeem us. Oh, we had hoped it would be another way." Saint Paul wrote to the Romans. He told them that he hoped to see them on his way to Spain. Going to Spain was his grand design, his great dream, his high hope. But Paul never got to Spain. Instead, his journey ended in a prison cell in Rome. He could not pull off what he saw in his mind.

It has been very well said that *every person dreams of one life and is forced to live another*. Such appears to have been true for Jesus, and yes, even for God! From the garden of Eden to the crucifixion, God seems to have had a grand dream for the human race but was forced to live another experience. Every person dreams of one life and is forced to live another.

39

Parents have dreams for their children. We all do. I always knew my children would be a cross between Albert Einstein, Tom Selleck, and Joe Montana. On the other hand, I'm certain that I'm not their ideal dream of a parent, either. I knew just how I'd be as a parent in my dreams. I'd be slim, popular, handsome, and very caring and understanding. I'd be up on their music, and kind and tolerant when they brought home poor grades. I'd spend hours communicating with my boys. We'd go down the road, arm-in-arm like Andy Taylor and Opie in Mayberry on the way to the fishing hole, and have these long, meaningful father-son talks. You dream one life and are forced to live another. It's enough to make you live only for momentary pleasure or admit the utter meaninglessness of life.

Here, it seems, is the essence of life. If indeed every person dreams of one life and is forced to live another, then the manner in which one repairs that dream and connects it with a lasting purpose has to be the greatest news in the world. The essence of the crucifixion and the resurrection of Jesus Christ is not solely to be found in a personal guarantee of life after death for you and me. The resurrection of Christ is an affirmation of a certain dream for life. The schematic designs of human evil were exposed and condemned for what they were. The central claim of the New Testament is the ultimate triumph of goodness. The resurrection is the triumph of a design for life that is upheld as the fundamental principle of the universe even if the world tries to crucify it.

Consequently, Saint Paul could affirm, "And we know that all things work together for good to them that love God, to them who are called according to His dream" (Romans 8:28). Here Paul is not saying that we all get to live the life of our dreams. A lot of things happen to us that are not good. We are indeed forced to live another kind of life at times. Paul *is* saying that if a person will consider all the experiences of his or her life, both the good and the bad, and bond them together with love for God, then the sum total of that life, the grand design of that person's history, will be good. As such, it is indeed possible to believe in the sun when it is not shining, to believe in love when you cannot directly feel it, and to believe in God when God is silent for a period. Even if the world crucifies you, the design of God's universe and your life with it will ultimately triumph. The dream will triumph even if it is not immediately evident.

You and I live by our dreams as much as by our particular experiences. In this limited world of broken dreams, in this world where we dream of one life and are forced to live another, a conclusion comes from resurrection. If God's dream for goodness triumphs, then one thing is certain: we can, indeed, live with the limits we have to face.

Failure is relative to time. No one really knows when he has succeeded or failed if all he does is look at the present.[16] God's design and God's time turn a lot of failures into successes. We must measure success by God's standard of design in history, not by whether or not we are immediately on the top of the world's heap. I know many people who have "arrived" and they are not very happy. I know others who look back on what they thought was a burden at the time and they now view it as having been a tremendous learning experience.

Consider the Reverend Kiyoshi Tanimoto. In 1944, he was the minister of the largest Protestant congregation in southern Japan. It was in the city of Hiroshima. Tanimoto must have been proud of his large church. Then one day, a yellow flash came. Mr. Tanimoto dove instinctively into a garden and wedged himself between two huge rocks. A powerful blast of wind and fire blew over him. It knocked him unconscious. When he came to and got on his feet, the city was flat as a desert. Sixty-eight thousand human beings were killed instantly. Only thirty members of his 3,500 member church were still alive. Rev. Tanimoto began to rebuild his crucified church. He arranged for the spiritual adoption of five hundred Hiroshima orphans by North American families. As a result of his work, all bomb survivors became eligible for free medical treatment. Rev. Tanimoto also created a Peace Foundation. In that Foundation's museum a little girl named Sadako placed two cranes made of folded paper. It was her belief that if a person who was ill made these little paper cranes, the person would get better. Well, Rev. Tanimoto died and little Sadako also died, after ten years of horrible suffering.[17] Two people who loved their enemies, whose righteousness was greater than the Pharisees, who were executed by forces they did not understand, cause us to ask, "Where was the design in all of this?" What happened to the dream? They believed in the sun when all they saw was a mushroom cloud that rose six miles high in only eight minutes. They believed in love when they could not feel it, and they believed in God when God was silent for a period. Naked, bleeding, hairless, and with skin hanging loose, they went to their early graves. They dreamed of one life and were forced to live another.

Today, thirty years after their death, a statue stands in Hiroshima. The statue was built in memory of their deaths. It is the figure of two children on either side and another child on top, their arms outstretched to express their hope for a peaceful world. For over thirty years, to this very day, Japanese children keep the center of that statue filled with many-colored paper cranes. It is the largest monument to peace in the history of the world. God's design of love holds. It stands. It triumphs for all generations over any design of darkness and death. Paul is absolutely correct. History has proved it in a thousand ways. If a person will consider all the experiences of his life and bond them together with love for God, then the sum total of that life will be good.

The design of God will ultimately triumph. From Bethlehem to Gethsemane to Calvary, the innocent do suffer. The good and the lonely often get what they do *not* deserve. But goodness never stays in the dark. The truth never stays crucified. The central theme in human history is the same as the central theme of the New Testament: *the ultimate triumph of goodness*. If we would but believe that, our lives would claim an unbelievable power and freedom. This power and freedom would give us some religious authenticity as we seek to live in a world of blind guides and ignorant professors.

Blind Guides And Ignorant Professors

During a recent fall break, my colleague, Professor Bill Cope, another friend and I went fishing off the Outer Banks of North

Carolina. We had been out in a boat about 10 miles from the channel. After a successful day, with our coolers full of fish and our bodies aching, we headed the boat back toward the mainland. As we followed the channel toward shallow water we saw a huge commotion speeding out of the channel toward the open water. A group of a dozen or more dolphins was breaking the water in a perfect circle. They were chattering incessantly in their high-pitched voices and swimming and diving at top speed. Many small fishing boats had stopped to watch the spectacle. The dolphins, still in a huge circle, weaved their way among the islands, staying right in the middle of the channel. We curiously puttered over to within 15 feet of the circle. All of a sudden a black mountain seemed to rise out of the circle and plunge down again, leaving a huge tail to slam the water. It was a whale, the largest living thing any of us had ever seen. It was almost seventy feet long. We hastily backed up. The last we saw of it, the whale was on a straight shot to the open ocean about five miles out to sea. And the dolphins were still leading it out.

This fortunate beast had become confused and gone into shallow water. His buddies, the dolphins, were guiding him to safety. They were faithfully doing what nature had given them the capacity to do. Without those guides, this powerful animal would have died.

Regardless of how strong and brilliant we humans become, we, too, become confused in life and have to turn to others to lead us away from shallow perceptions and ways of thinking. More often than not our guides tend to be our religious leaders and our professors. Teachers and preachers are supposed to be people who know much and have wisdom that can help us solve problems. If you can't follow your priests, preachers, and teachers, whom *can* you follow?

How amazing and startling it is to find in the New Testament a reference to *blind* guides and *ignorant* professors. The terms appear to be oxymorons. Who would want to hire a guide that is blind? Who would be foolish enough to pay money to study under a professor who is ignorant?

43

Romans 2:17-24 is not a good scripture for preachers and teachers. We would do well to avoid it. But the scripture is there. It must be articulated. Not only is it there but it has a ring of contemporary relevance even though it comes from an ancient setting. The church has always had problems with the moral blindness and intellectual foolishness of its priests, preachers, and teachers.

In our day when the faith of many has been rocked by the child abuse and materialistic greed of preachers and teachers, this scripture screams at us. Blind guides and ignorant professors. There are Catholic priests and bishops being indicted for having molested children, Protestant evangelists in jail for fraud, and professors earning over $100,000 a year from church-related institutions who have never taught a course there. They have simply sold their name.

Any contemporary discussion about living in a limited world must honestly wrestle with the limited influence of traditional religious images. So bogus has become the image of religion in the eyes of many citizens that the symbols of religion are fair game for the entertainment industry. I sat with my wife and college-aged son at a Jimmy Buffett concert in Raleigh, North Carolina. It was a wonderful concert, attended by over 40,000 devoted fans, myself included.

When the fabulous Buffett reached a certain segment of his song "Fruitcakes," the crowd with me good-naturedly started poking and pointing. The words are simple but true: "Religion, religion, oh there's a thin line / Between Saturday night and Sunday morning."[18] The song goes on to talk about the dishonesty of preachers and notes that religion is in the hands of some strange people. But the actual truth is that nothing is as simple as these religious people try to make it.

The words of the song were as haunting to me as they are true. Each semester I teach a course titled Religion 119, Christian Worship. Students who attend nine of the fourteen worship services in our chapel and produce a final paper about the experience, writing essays on certain questions, can receive one hour of semester course credit. To date, over 600 students have written these papers in the past five years. And as I read papers I always discern a familiar pattern. About one-third of the students will have stopped attending church prior to college. And the number one reason given for their lack of a religious background will be this: their parents dropped out of church over the hypocrisy of someone who pretended to be a guide or teacher. The preacher ran off with the choir director or a secretary. Or the venerable church school teacher or deacon got arrested for embezzlement. Or some arrogant born-again Christian kept putting on the pressure, looking for the speck of sawdust in their parents' moral behavior while ignoring the plank of smug self-righteousness sticking out of his own eye. So their parents quit church and that meant they stopped taking the children. It's an old but true story.

Let's look at the preacher or priest. How do we view these spiritual guides, these people who talk to us from pulpits? I'm amazed at the mystique associated with clergy. Every fall those of us who follow sports hear much about the Notre Dame mystique as it applies to their football team. The mystique is now enhanced by a movie titled *Rudy*. The movie focuses on this little, tough fellow whose goal in life is to play for Notre Dame. It chronicles his dedication and hard work, both athletically and academically. And, indeed, the real-life drama concludes with Rudy playing a play in a game and being carried off the field on his teammates' shoulders.

I spoke in South Bend, Indiana, some years ago. And the experience reminded me of a mystique that is common to most of us. As part of the speaking engagement's requirements I had to be the guest on an early morning television talk show. The station was WSJV, Channel 28, South Bend. The show came on right after *Good Morning America*. It was called *Good Morning Michiana*. I was doing a forum entitled "How to Be a Minister and a Human Being." Like past forum keynote speakers I had to sit on a couch with the talk show host and á la the Larry King Show take telephone calls from people in that part of Michigan and Indiana. I dreaded it. I just knew some professors would call in questions I couldn't answer. Or worse yet, some nut would call in a crazy question and get me in a trap that would demand an answer certain to antagonize half the viewers. The interview began with the host asking me, "Uh, what shall I call you: Doctor, Father, Reverend or Preacher Warlick?" Rather innocently I said, "I prefer to be called Hal."

You would have thought I had struck him between the eyes with a club. He said, "Oh, I could never call a Holy Man by his first name." The television switchboard immediately lit up like a Christmas tree. That's all we dealt with the whole show: the mystique embodied in what you call or don't call a supposed Holy Person. I never knew how many people's sensitivities were offended or affirmed by calling someone by his first name.

From Chicago to East Lansing the viewers were at it. Who is this person who declares God can speak through him or her?

Is the person a man, woman, or a myth?

Is the person a saint or a sinner?

Are we talking to a conversion artist or a con artist?

Are you a spiritual shepherd or an ecclesiastical pimp?

A missionary or a mercenary?

Are we receiving tithes and offerings or just stealing in the name of the Lord?

At some point in life we have to address these issues. What better place than in discussing life's limits? Robes can't hide us from what's underneath. And a collar on backwards cannot shield us from reality.

One of the problems with clergy is the holy person myth. Many people will accept ludicrous misrepresentations of reality from these people because they faithfully believe that these leaders have been set aside from ordinary humans. Somehow the myth states that these people have moral perfection, freedom from temptation and sin, and are possessed with special wisdom. As such, they speak of God, know God, and can make things right *for us* with God.

If you read the Bible you will note that most of its leading religious figures are not holy men or women at all. To be certain, they are not flagrantly immoral, insane, or uncouth. They do keep their noses relatively clean. And, like most preachers and teachers today, they are some of the finest people you could ever meet. But

46

they are all human. They all live with limits. And, like today, the dangerous ones are those who believe in the myth that they are somehow immune from human temptation and realities, that they have no limits with which to grapple theologically.

One of the most important aspects of an education is learning to see our leaders, whether governmental, religious, or educational, for what they are: imperfect human beings. Conversely, if we can learn to have faith in the political process, the church, and in education in spite of setbacks to our myths about preachers, teachers, and politicians, then we have learned much. Leaders are people who require the input, the knowledge, and the challenge of people just like you and me. When we stand back and allow the clergy, the professors, and the politicians to make all our decisions for us we are in trouble. Not only do we follow, but we help create blind guides and ignorant professors.

This is not easy to do. All of us want reassurance that there are no mysteries to trouble the mind. We like being told, "Only believe. These are the facts." Crowds follow the person who announces very confidently, "It's all so very simple. Come hear the answers. One, two, three, four. Now, I have told you what to do. Go and do it!"

The Bible was not afraid to explode this myth. It had to. Those who claimed to know the way had suddenly lost the way. But they were still serving as guides and professors.

The messages of Jesus and Paul are not just aimed at professional preachers and teachers. They are aimed at everyone who fancies himself or herself a devout believer. You and I live in an era when it has become in vogue, that is, popular, to tell people, "I am a born-again Christian. I'm saved. I've got it made. And here is how I can help you. It's all so very simple. One, two, three, four. Now that I have told you how to do it, you go and do it! It's simple and no limits are involved."

In short, when you are involved in the religious enterprise in any way that puts you in the limelight, you better be careful there isn't a ditch waiting for you just around the corner.

The words of Paul to the Romans would translate this way in the modern vernacular. "You call yourself a Christian. You think you've got it made because you've got Jesus. And not only that, but you brag about your relationship with God and how much scripture you know and how many Sunday School certificates you have and how you can pray. You think of those who don't believe as you believe as blind and you think it's your duty to guide them? You think of other people as foolish people and you think it is your responsibility to be their teacher? Well, if I'm not mistaken, in spite of your arrogance, there's a skeleton or two in your closet. You have become a blind guide and an ignorant professor when you do not live with your limits."

When we get right down to it, the apostle Paul and Jesus, especially in his teaching about people who see the speck of sawdust in others' eyes but avoid the plank in their own, are correct. In order for religion to have any authenticity, at some point integrity has to be possessed. The first thing that occurs whenever the world discovers the blind leading the blind and the ignorant teaching the foolish is that the world calls into question the sincerity of the entire enterprise.

Have you ever been on a trip or a hike with a really competent guide? A good guide is someone who knows the territory but doesn't make you feel like a fool for not knowing it. A competent guide is more concerned with what you experience than what he or she experiences. A good guide is more concerned with the safety of others than his own ability to impress.

And have you ever had a really good professor or teacher? Have you ever noticed that the good professors appear to know less than the mediocre professors? If they don't know something, the good professors say, "That's a good question. I don't know the answer." The mediocre teachers make up an answer.

We are all guides and teachers to one another. If not, we shall one day perform those roles for our children, our employees and occasionally even our loved ones. In our kind of world we may have to be religious guides to one another in a time when religion itself has lost its lofty place in the repertoire of human imagery. The signs may be limited, if there at all.

No Signs

The so-called experts tell us that we often form our opinion of someone in the first five seconds after we first meet him. Consequently they teach that the signs one gives off in the first five seconds of a job interview determine whether he or she will get the job. They contend that a person is greatly judged by appearance.

Students are aware of this. Watch a group of college students get ready to interview for a job. They don ties and jackets and long dresses. Some even shave their semester-long beard or cut their slightly long hair. The same holds true for rush week among fraternities and sororities. One often sees attractive 21-year-old ladies trying to wobble on high heels from a residence hall to the Campus Center. And some of the white dresses obviously haven't been worn since high school.

We are a world that looks for "signs" as to what is going on. "Is your child not eating right, not sleeping right, becoming more withdrawn, and so forth? That may be a sign that he or she is having experiences with drugs." At least that's what the commercial says. Signs are important.

Signs are certainly important in the business and political worlds. Not only do *people* have vital signs, such as pulse rates and blood pressure, but we are told that the economy has vital signs, political campaigns have vital signs and even universities have vital signs which measure their relative health or sickness.

Sometimes our infatuation with signs becomes almost silly. I once taught a course at Harvard University on organizational development. We utilized case studies from the Harvard Business School, CEOs from IBM and Polaroid, and a host of guest lecturers. I'll never forget some of the experiences when these hot shot corporate experts blew into the classroom. Based on the theory that people pick up our "signs" of professional competency in the first five seconds of a meeting, I had several guests who gave astounding lectures on "dressing for success." The basic premise was that how you dress gives a sign that communicates how you feel about yourself and who you are.

49

I sat in amazement as I listened to one "expert" tell my students how an executive woman should dress for success. The lecture went something like this. If your male colleagues wear dark blue or gray suits, white or blue long-sleeved shirts and subtle ties, then you should dress in outfits where the jackets and skirts are matching material. If the men wear sports coats with contrasting slacks, then you can mix and match your wardrobe, too. Even if the image is different from your personality, you should adopt it if you wish to succeed. *Your goal is to make money*, even if you have to compromise your dress during the work day in order to meet your goal. It's all a part of the game. You want to exhibit the right "signs." When you land your first job, borrow two or three thousand dollars from the bank to buy a new wardrobe. Camel, gray, black, navy, white or beige in a solid color are most acceptable. Buying that expensive wardrobe will be one of the keys to your success. Quality clothes help make the executive. They help you give off the right sign!

Then, as the students and I sat in open-mouthed silence, came the real zinger: "Always wear sunglasses when it's bright outdoors, for you want to avoid squinting, which causes premature crow's-feet."

Good grief. Here were students paying many hard-earned dollars in tuition alone to go to that university, and a high-priced person from the business world was telling them their success really didn't depend on that education. It depended on wearing sunglasses to keep from getting premature *crow's-feet*.

Are we serious? Are the "signs" of accomplishment really accounting for personal and professional success? Do we give authority to people according to the signs we see? Apparently so. Our generation has witnessed the remarkable marketing of bogus signs. A $35.00 fake Rolex watch can be bought on any street corner in downtown Manhattan. The weight of the wristband and the movement of the second hand are the only differences which distinguish it from the real thing. Oh, as I found out a few years ago when I had one, after six months the fake Rolex watch stops running and the cheap metal wristband puts a green ring around your wrist. But, hey, for six months I looked very important. And,

God bless Taiwan, they now have helped us all. There is a fake cellular-one car phone. That's right, friends, some of the cars you see riding around town with apparent car phones in them, don't have a car phone at all. But it looks good. Some people are just naive enough to reason that an insurance agent, a salesman, or even a preacher who has a car phone must be more successful and carry more authority than one who doesn't have one. We look for the right "sign" more than we'd care to admit. *We need signs as vindication of a person's authority.*

One day Jesus Christ encountered the same phenomenon. He was in debate with some Pharisees. The Pharisees asked Jesus to supply "a sign from heaven." It was a logical request to the Son of God. Comedian Woody Allen used to say, for example, that he would believe in God if God would give him a sign, like a million dollar deposit in Allen's name in a Swiss bank account.

The Pharisees weren't out of step to ask Jesus for a sign of His authority. Who wants to believe in a Messiah so limited he or she can't produce a sign of divine proof?

Apparently signs had been given before. When Moses approached Pharaoh as the spokesman of God and demanded the freeing of the slaves, Pharaoh wanted a "sign." Moses turned his rod into a snake and Nile water into blood. Pharaoh was obviously impressed by these signs which demonstrated Moses' authority.

In like manner, Elijah went before King Ahab to denounce his part in Baal-worship in Israel. Elijah announced three years' drought as a sign of God's power. Since Baal was supposed to be the rain-giver god, this sign hit Baal right in the kisser.

Didn't the Pharisees have a right to expect a similar sign from Jesus as proof of *His* status? Apparently this request, *coming from religious people*, really angered Jesus. It really angered Him.

Why did religious people, who were supposed to believe in God, need signs to believe in Him? Was not Jesus Himself "sign" enough? External signs may have been necessary for a heathen Pharaoh or a back-sliding king. But why couldn't religious people decide without the aid of signs whether Jesus' teaching was true or not? So Jesus responded, "Why does this evil generation seek a

51

sign? Truly, I say to you, no sign shall be given to this generation …" (Mark 8:12).[19]

It remains a pivotal issue for our generation. Why do Christians need signs? Isn't Jesus' life and death enough sign for us? Can the proclamation of the kingdom and the cross stand as enough evidence? In essence, Jesus maintained that if believers have to have signs, then no sign will convince that person of God's authority. The "sign" will never be authoritative enough. How much money would God have to raise as God's sign? Oral Roberts once said eleven million dollars. How many cures would God have to work?

Are we so evil that we need a sign? Are we so incapable of living with limits that faith without certainty is impossible?

Let me illustrate from personal experience. I was standing in the checkout line of a Boston bookstore where I knew the manager. He stopped me and said, "I've got a check I need for you to vouch for. We normally don't take checks, but this man rummaging through the used books back there says you know him and can reference him. He doesn't have any cash. He's very polite. Is it okay to take his check?" I looked back and there, in his usual attire of blue jeans and rumpled sweater, was Charles Merrill on his hands and knees rummaging through used books. Charles Merrill of Merrill, Lynch, Pierce can dress any way he wants to and usually does. I said, "Yes, you can take his check. And if he decides to give you another one to buy the building and turn it into a K-Mart, you can take that one, too." Charles Merrill doesn't have to worry about camel, gray, black or navy suits. He doesn't even have to worry about whether or not he gets premature crow's-feet. He has all the authority and money he needs. He doesn't need any of the "signs." *He doesn't even have to play the game, if he doesn't want to. Now that's real authority.*

Let me bring the issue closer to home. I used to write all over a good student's paper or test booklet. I wrote copious comments, paragraph after paragraph. Suddenly it dawned on me that all I need to write is "Excellent," A+. A good student knows it is good. By contrast, if the student doesn't know why it's excellent, it probably isn't excellent.

52

Consider how our world operates both with and without signs. In some public buildings there are signs prohibiting smoking. But in church sanctuaries no such signs are needed. Who would light up and smoke a cigarette during a church service? The nature of the building and the character of the service make it unnecessary to post a no-smoking sign in there. The church can live with the limitation of not having a sign prohibiting smoking because of its identity.

In fact, our freedom, our honor, and much of what is dear to us in life depend on acts that do not have to be enforced by signs. *Consider the home.* Out in the business world a wage and hour schedule is often posted by law. Gratuity information is printed on the menu — "parties of six or more will have fifteen percent gratuity added to the bill." Terms of employment statutes are posted in factories and speed limit signs control the highways. But consider the home. Can you imagine going into a home and seeing a sign which states the number of hours that mother will put in for a sick child? Can you imagine a sign posted in a living room which says, "Family will pay up to $10,000 for emergency surgery for any one of its members?" If you need a sign for things like that, I'd advise you to find another family. Certainly a family is bound together in spite of outward limits on its legalistic obligations.

This is what prompted Jesus' reaction to the Pharisees. People live by faith and not by signs. If you need positive signs to hold your faith together or to enforce it, then it isn't much of a faith. If Jesus Christ has to be equated with some particular political, economic, or medical sign in order to have some authority, that isn't much authority at all. Jesus Christ has been in all kinds of societies, living under all kinds of political systems, in all kinds of bodies. God has lived in democracies, and God has lived in the hearts of people under dictatorships. God does not have to bend anything to anyone's particular tastes in order to have authority. God can dress any way God wants to dress. People tend to want to point to "signs" that Jesus is the sole possession and monopoly of a certain class with a particular point of view.

53

Jesus knew that. "No signs," he countered. No signs? Well, what are we to do when people exclaim, "Look, here He is. There He goes. Yonder He is"?

Do believers need a sign? If I interpret this scripture correctly, "No, they don't." *In fact, one of the grandest stages in Christianity is that moment when a person can simply but profoundly state, "Lord, I believe. That's all I need."*

When you are in love, your girlfriend or boyfriend starts off giving you little signs of affection. Sometimes we reach the point of craving a letter, a card, a flower, as a sign that he "loves" me. But any true love, any intimate relationship, in the long run must reach a point where you know the person is your love even if there is no sign of it. Otherwise, instead of love, the relationship would be built on goose-stepping for favors.

Only those who live with limits can truly understand the meaning of "faith." We preachers not only come from a tradition which revels in dreams, insights, and signs but we enter our profession through a "call." We focus on words, speeches, and calls. Perhaps we can theologically appropriate limited signs. But limited calls? What do we do to keep the fires of faith flickering among the faithful when it appears to a modern-day world that God is severely limiting God's calls to humankind? Can we live with limited revelation?

No Calls

You and I live in the world of the telephone. Analysts tell us that most of us will spend two years of our lives on the telephone. Most likely they will not be the best two years.

Calling a college student has changed dramatically since I was in school. Over two-thirds of our students now have answering machines with recorded messages. This week I sat down to call some students. Here's what I got: "Hi, this is Page and Kathy's room. We are not here right now, but leave a message and we'll get back to you." According to our Dean of Student Affairs, "A telephone answering machine is almost standard equipment for today's college student."

And older adults are no different. Last month my office telephone bill had 51 long distance calls of less than twenty seconds to answering machines.

Ah, the age of the telephone. We of all people can ask, "Why doesn't God talk anymore?"

I mean, God called Moses through a burning bush. God placed a call to Abraham through three wandering strangers. God phoned Samuel late at night in a dream. God placed a call to Jacob down a long ladder. God whispered to Elijah on Mount Horeb. We have AT&T, Sprint, MCI, CNN, and a host of other companies. It would be so easy for God to place a call or give an interview. If Jesus came "in the fullness of time," what about now? Wouldn't everyone pause and lend an ear if God used the telephone just once and called earth?

In Tennessee Williams' play *Sweet Bird of Youth*, the heckler says to Miss Lucy, "I believe that the silence of God, the absolute speechlessness of God, is a long, long and awful thing..." The late Carlyle Marney retired from his church in Charlotte and went to Wolf Pen Mountain. There he waited for God to say something. He confessed that he had figured that if he could get some time completely free from his preaching, his church work, and his worldly obligations that God would really jabber. After five years of waiting, hiking, hoeing, splitting wood, sleeping, praying and studying, he finally reasoned that God had had ample time. But the inscrutable silence simply pushed him back on resources, memories and ideals he already had. With great certainty he said, *"It's as if God has said all God intends to say."*[20]

I can identify with the confusion. Our family owns a small farm and house in Davidson County. I go out there to work on sermons and be by myself. I've prayed, meditated, weeded the garden, watered the flowers, cut the grass, sat in the dark, removed myself from 36 channels of cable television and local newspapers. *I haven't heard much.* Maybe I don't have enough faith. Have you ever felt that way?

The writer of Hebrews makes a claim: "When in former times God spoke to our forefathers, he spoke in fragmentary and varied fashion through the prophets. But in this, the final age, God has spoken to us in the son" (1:1-2).

The biblical witness insists that God speaks, that God does talk. It begins in the angel's visit to Mary about the birth of Christ. In plain language the angel says, "Mary, God has been using various instruments to try to communicate to the world, but they haven't been working too well. God has been speaking to all these prophets for generations. But as many times as he has tried to reveal himself, humans haven't listened too well. Sometimes people barked, 'Who's this?' Other times whole societies hung up on him. Then again, some shrewd manipulators put God on hold and proceeded to speak for God. So, Mary, you are highly favored, because God has decided to hang up the telephone, cease these fragmentary and varied little conversations, and open up and tell it all. No more phone calls. No more recorded messages. God is going to make a personal visit and God needs some transportation, a vehicle to get here, or all those humans will hang up on God or say they're out to lunch again. God's going to really jabber this time. He's coming and you are going to be the person to help God get the message across."

A child was born. God opened up and wrote an autobiography in the life of God's son.

Now, amazingly enough, no sooner did this child get here and start talking than he began to talk about leaving.

Consider the sequence. God had previously talked to us only in fragments and in varied fashion through these people named Abraham, Moses, Jacob, Elijah, and all the rest. It wasn't clear enough. Too much static on the line. So God said, "I'm going to come down there and open up and bare it all." And God did. But as God revealed Godself the message led to the cross. Those people who stayed with this child of God and heard Him speak went through an emotional roller coaster. They saw Him confront the religious establishment, raise people from the dead, and love people as none had before. Then it all turned to despair. Bethlehem's child, the hope of the world, was crudely crucified. They fled the scene in disgust and desolation. Then when they were on the bottom with their emotions, He came back and started speaking again.

Their emotions went right back to the top. They were singing and laughing and applauding. One writer said they stayed in the church singing praises to God *for three days*. Then Jesus talked about leaving and God's being silent again. *He told them that if He were to stay and keep talking they would be limited, but if He departed they would be expanded in their gospel.*

What on earth does that mean? Wouldn't we truly be better off with Jesus around talking or at least placing a few person-to-person telephone calls?

James Stuart of Edinburgh used to say that Jesus had to leave in order that our religion would be spiritualized. Apparently Jesus wanted a religion that is a matter of experience and not of appearance or language.

Jesus' words to His disciples are quite clear. They are recorded in John's gospel: "… you are filled with grief. But I tell you the truth: It is for your good that I am going away. Unless I go away, the Counselor will not come to you; but if I go, I will send him to you" (John 16:6-7, NIV).

Jesus was talking about the danger of hanging around too long or sending messages too often. My friend Tom Downing[21] conjectured what probably would have happened had Jesus lived to a ripe old age. His followers would have become a little band of groupies running around in the kindergarten of their faith until the day they died. Every time there was a dilemma in their lives they would have gone to Jesus and asked, "What do we do now?" Like the followers of the Rajneesh or Jim Jones or the Dalai Lama, they would have relied on appearance and words, instead of their own experience with God.

Even with Jesus' early death that happened for a period of time. When Saint John died there were ten Christian churches in the Holy Land. Three hundred years later there were 24 churches in the Holy Land. Also at the time John died there were two churches in Italy and twenty in Asia Minor. But 300 years later whereas the ten Holy land churches had grown to 24, the two in Italy had grown to 77 churches and the twenty in Asia had grown to 165 churches.

Why? Obvious answer. The Holy Land churches had the disciples, their families, and their descendants in them. Every time there was a dilemma, they just went to some descendant of the original group and asked, "What do we do now?" And, for three hundred years every time they got a new idea or revelation I imagine many in the Holy Land heard the seven famous last words of the church: "We've never done it that way before."

Jesus' words were prophetic: "It's for your good that I'm going away and not talking anymore. From now on the Holy Spirit will speak through your experiences."

God speaks. God still speaks. But it is in the experiences we humans have with Him. Herein lies a genuine theological concern. In a world of dim visions, blind guides, limited signs, and far less than open communication with God, how can we open ourselves to receive genuine Christian experiences?

Perhaps the place to begin is with a radical reappraisal of our own lifestyles. If communication with God is, indeed, more limited than in certain periods of heightened spirituality, then we must consider comfort, procrastination and traditional road maps as impediments rather than guides to the Holy. Much of our inability to live with the perceived limitations placed upon us eventuated from our failure to distinguish illusion from reality.

Chapter Three

Illusion Or Reality?

Back in the mid 1970s to early 1980s hypnosis was viewed as a major cure for many of society's ills. If you had a problem with being overweight, smoking cigarettes, drinking too much, or being a juvenile delinquent, many professional hypnotists would, for a hefty fee, offer their services to hypnotize your problems away.

The church I pastored in Texas at the time contained among its members some overweight women with a passion for improving their bodies. These women had apparently tried everything they could to lose weight: diets, exercise, weeks at fashionable fat farms, and the like. None of the "cures" seemed to last. They'd go off the diets, quit exercising, abandon the principles learned at the fat farm, and balloon up to their old weight. Finally, one of my friends discovered a hypnotist in Houston who would hypnotize the problem away. She sent in her $150.00 registration fee, drove to Houston, and entered a rented high school gymnasium.

Over 220 people were seated in reclining chairs facing the stage. The hypnotist gave what appeared to be a stimulating and spontaneous speech. Then he put everyone under and finally reawakened them. My friend decided she would stay and repeat the session. After the next wave of people filled the reclining chairs she was amazed to learn that instead of being a spontaneous speech, the hypnotist's speech was as canned as corn. Obviously the remedy did not take for any of the participants. It's been fifteen years now and the participants I know, including myself, are just as overweight as ever.

I don't blame them for trying, though. When I was struggling to pass French in college, I bought a tape player and some audio tapes to study French. The promise was that you could go to sleep with the tape running and your earphones on and the message would go into your brain all night. I did that the night before the final exam. I made a *D*, as in "dog," on that exam.

Now psychologists have changed dramatically their value of hypnosis. *De-hypnosis* is now in vogue. In fact, psychologists tell me that the greatest problem we have in society is illusion. They say that television and fantasy have become so much a part of our lives that most people expect to live in la-la land and are walking around spaced out. We as a society seem to have lost touch with reality. We have let an entertainment world cause us to live with illusions instead of reality. We see illusions of sex on television and we are shocked when men and women don't act like that in real life. We conjure up images and illusions of perfection and get divorced when reality and its people aren't perfect. We want our teachers to be like Robin Williams, our wives to be like Meryl Streep, our boyfriends to be like Mel Gibson, and our girlfriends to be like Cindy Crawford in heat. We live in such a world of illusion that reality would kill even our national politicians: George Bush had to maintain the illusion that we were not in a recession and Bill Clinton has to maintain the illusion that he really did not dodge the Vietnam War. To face reality would be defeat in the political realm.

Herein seems to be a genuine clue for understanding how to hear the voice of God and live a Christian life in today's world. We must accept the limitations of reality, of being human.

One of the main messages of the Bible, it appears to me, is the horrible way evil works through illusion. From the very beginning Adam and Eve can't accept the reality of their limitations and even in paradise give in to the illusion that they can eat the forbidden fruit and get away with it.

The story of the rich man and Lazarus appeals to me because it's about illusion and reality. The rich man is living a fantasy life. He's so wrapped up in the false world of his affluence that he can't even see the reality of the poor beggar, Lazarus, at his very gate. Even his religion has put him in a fantasy world and protected him from reality. Most rich people's religion is a comforting *illusion.* That's one reason Jesus said it's easier for a camel to go through the eye of a needle than a rich person to enter the Kingdom of God. The more we accumulate and achieve in life the farther that seems to take us from the reality of how the rest of the world lives. Even our religion becomes illusion — a way of escape from the harsh, brutal realities of human existence.

Religion can be a useful *illusion.* It can uplift, inspire, encourage, and produce calmness in the midst of stress. But Jesus Christ had some harsh things to say about religion which never goes beyond inner feelings and from first-to-last serves as a built-in emotional device to provide people the illusion of comfort in a cruel and unjust world. He called such people "fools" and was harder on them than on sinners. "Fool, get real, this night your soul is required of you. Fool, get real, you did not visit the sick, visit the prisoner, feed the hungry, clothe the naked, take care of the widowed." "Fool, get real," he said over and over again.

Lest we pick on religion, look at other modern-day illusions. Science can become an illusion. "Technology will save us" is the cry. It can save us from this cruel and unjust world. We can learn the properties of radium by suitable laboratory tests. We can operate with lasers. We can apply the scientific method to everything. We can build bigger rockets and explore space. We can solve our problems with synthetic foods, energy resources and the like. "Fool, get real." The gas chambers in Nazi Germany were built by learned engineers. People were shot to death by firing squads composed of college professors. Little children were dashed to death by registered nurses. "Fool, get real."

Ah, but surely humanism will save us. Enough social programs will take care of the alcoholics, the drug addicts, and the homeless. And if they won't, surely morality will. If everyone has a course like Self, Society, and Moral Decision-making, coupled with knowledge of Self, Society, and World, won't that be enough? Morality is strong in principle. But it's an illusion not to know it's weak in power. The apostle Paul and Martin Luther had powerful minds and great wills, but the more they tried to apply their morality to their passions, the more they were overwhelmed. Morality is an illusion. "Fool, get real."

One of the most celebrated liars in the history of the world was Baron von Munchhausen. The Baron could really tell them. He was so good at fantasy that he got away with most of his lies. One of his big lies concerned an experience he had while walking in a bog. The Baron claimed he fell into quicksand. When he had sunk up to his neck and the situation looked desperate, he said he worked the miracle by grabbing his hair with his hands and pulling himself out.[22] Some of our illusions in the face of our human predicament sound equally absurd.

The Bible appeals to me because it is such a realistic book. The Bible is not a book on moral philosophy. It is not a collection of vague ethical principles. It is not a science book. It is not even a history book. Even if every word of it were true historical fact, that would not be enough. Perhaps you have read that one weekend 600 neo-Nazis marched in Dresden, Germany, and that arsonists attacked a Holocaust memorial. German Chancellor Helmut Kohl, angry and surrounded by police, stopped and shouted at the demonstrators, "You have learned nothing from our history! This is pure Nazism." No, my friends, even when we have historical facts in hand, beautiful monuments, and eyewitnesses, we humans still cannot pull ourselves out of our messes by our own hair. We Christians have proved this. Those who believe the Bible is literally and historically true are the most intolerant, most unloving, and most unaccepting people we have. They appear to learn little from what they believe to be historically true. Those who are pro-life tend to be anti-welfare and *for* capital punishment. Those who are anti-capital punishment tend to be pro-abortion.

Our Bible proclaims a God and what that God is able to do: set captives free and lead those who sit in darkness into light. It is about a Savior who came not to edify but to save us from our sins. It is about a disturbing Savior who said, "He that hates his brothers and sisters is in darkness and walks in darkness." This Bible is about reality, not illusion.

We can study science and history and we must. We can study morals and we must. We can get to know a foreign language by amassing its vocabulary and studying its syntax and we must. But *we cannot get to know a person except by loving him or her and there is no exception to this rule.* We have to get real about this and de-hypnotize ourselves.

The Bible deals primarily with reality: we do not pull ourselves out of our messes with our own hands. It's an illusion to think we can. We do not live unto ourselves. It's an illusion to think we can. We do not get to know people except by loving them. It's an illusion to think we can do otherwise.

One day at dusk, Moses herded his flock toward a sheltered place for the night. He saw a blazing bush and experienced the living God. He heard a voice that called him by name. Startled and fearful, Moses' trembling voice responded, "Here am I."

Then the Lord God said to Moses, "Put off your shoes ... for the place on which you are standing is holy ground." So Moses loosened his sandals and kicked them from his feet.

Now, that's strange — "Put *off* your shoes!" If it's holy ground wouldn't you want someone to put *on* his shoes? You cannot go in McDonald's barefooted today. Shoes are designed to protect. Shoes are designed to protect the feet from the rough rigors of the road.

Put *off* your shoes, Moses. Feel the bare dirt. Get real, Moses. We're going to deal with reality here, old boy. Being a wealthy, arrogant Egyptian, jumping on someone and murdering him, wasn't reality. Being a comfortable, retired shepherd living off your retirement fund isn't reality. Put off your shoes and let your feet hit the ground; I'm sending you back into the real world. Get all the cushions off your feet, Moses. This is holy ground and holy ground is real life. Learn to live among these limits and see God in them.

There is always the danger that our support systems of money, education, science, technology, and even religion, which cushion our lives, may insulate us so securely that all our thoughts, feelings, and expressions will become such a la-la dream world that we will cease to recognize the reality of the world we actually live in.

The Illusion Of The Crowd

One of the graphic illusions played out in our world as it heads toward its twenty-first century is that of religion as a herd phenomenon. We live in the age of the Mega-Church. We seem to have as much a passion for programs as we do for life itself. From children's ministries to senior adult trips, we seem to demand special programs that assure us that from birth to grave we will be part of a herd.

One spring I had an opportunity to teach for a few days in the World Arts and Cultures program at the University of California at Los Angeles, better known as UCLA. One of those classes was to be co-taught by a popular film director. This particular class lasted four hours, from 4 p.m. to 8 p.m. It met in a huge lecture hall and there were about one hundred students there. The format was interesting: we would see a movie, after which the director would point out the fine points in the camera work and facial expressions of the actors and actresses. I would then lecture on the religious symbols in the movie.

When the lights came back on after the movie, the teacher/movie director came over to me and said, "Would you mind if two of my actresses sat in the back of the room with you and worked on a script? They have heard what I have to say and are just here to listen to your talk." Well, when he motioned the two ladies over, I almost fell out of my seat. They were two of the tallest and most beautiful blondes I had ever seen. And they were dressed very scantily. This was truly Hollywood. Even a middle-aged chaplain from High Point recognized near perfection in its human form. I smiled at my good fortune. They introduced themselves and turned to back into their seats on either side of me. I almost fell out of my seat a second time.

Each actress had a large, ornate *tattoo* on her shoulder blade. I literally sat there transfixed by those tattoos. Young women just did not do that when I was their age. I must have been obvious in my staring at them. Every now and then they would look up and smile. Underneath I imagine they were saying to themselves, "Boy, is this hick from North Carolina behind the times."

Perhaps I am. If you watched the 1992 Olympics you saw several members of the U.S.A. swim team with a tattoo on their shoulder. And the U.S.A. women's volleyball team, almost to a girl, went out and had the olympic symbol, the interlocking rings, tattooed on their ankles.

Tattooing is an age-old and world-wide practice. Puncturing the skin with indelible scars and dyes is as ancient as any form of human identity. This peculiar and significant custom of primitive humans obviously still survives among us.

The forty-ninth chapter of the prophet Isaiah describes a name tattooed (engraved) on the palms of one's hands. Here was a prophet struggling to describe the love of God. His first thought, his first draft of the paper, you might say, was to conceive of God's love as strong, tender, and sacrificial — like a mother's love. But Isaiah was not happy with his first impression. Not every woman who gives birth to a child and becomes a mother loves the child in that way. So Isaiah abandoned his rough draft. Like a student who needs a writing fellow and decides the first few pages aren't good enough and crumples them up and fires them into the trash can, Isaiah was stumped. Where would he find some parallel in human experience that could adequately portray the strong, unfaltering, eternal love of God for humans?[23]

Suddenly Isaiah had a flame of vision. He saw a man with a name tattooed on the palms of his hands. Now this tattoo was not on his arm or shoulder blade or calf where it would be conspicuous to others on occasion, but in the hollow of the hand. It could only be seen by the person's own eyes.

That image is as bold as any image of God in the scriptures. The prophet wrote his final draft. To all humans who conceived of themselves as forsaken by friends, society, and even God, Isaiah conceived of God opening His hands and showing them to us and saying, "Behold, I have tattooed your name on my palms."

It's a great image, isn't it? No matter how alone and cut off we might feel, God has our name tattooed on God's palms. Actually it is a knowledge that should give us the courage to be alone, to be by ourselves at times, and still feel secure in our Christian lifestyle.

If there is a crying need in our time it is for us contemporary Americans to learn how to be alone. Most of us hate to be alone. We need a walkman, a portable CD player, a car telephone, a VCR or a watchman. Some of us even have to have a beer in our hand at a social function or throw our lives into food or sex. Anything to keep us from being alone. At times we have a lot in common with the character in this parable called the prodigal son. The more unhappy, alone, and lost the son feels, the more he celebrates, parties, and throws himself into the company of "friends." *He diverts himself from his loneliness.* He can no longer stand being alone; he must have something going on all the time. He cannot stand to be alone; he must have diversions.[24]

Because he cannot be alone, he is actually a prisoner. He is a prisoner to his homesickness, so he must constantly amuse himself. If there's a party, he is at it. If there's a video machine, it's got his quarters. If there's a keg, he's tapped it. *He can't be alone or he'd be homesick.* He cannot live with the limits of his aloneness.

He is a prisoner to his urges, so he must satisfy them. If you want to have sex, then he's there and ready. He carries condoms like some carry their driver's license. He can't be without sex or he'd have to face his urges.

He is a prisoner to a grand style of living and cannot let it go. He's always got to associate with the right kind of people or else he'd have to face his own true self.

His friends look at him and see this imposing free person — so independent of family and authority and education and principles. What a splendid and exciting fellow. The world only sees his diversions, the stuff he chooses to put in the show window of his life. What a facade. He appears to be a free person, but he's a prisoner to his diversions. *He cannot be alone and face himself.*

That's too great a limitation, so he must live with his illusions of sociability.

One of the most important ingredients in life is learning how to be alone at times with yourself. Unless you can turn your back occasionally on your diversions and retreat from them you will become cynical and disappointed. The person who cannot be alone occasionally loses his or her perspective of his own life. Troubles get magnified all out of proportion.

You see, if we are dependent on our diversions we get hypersensitive to our surroundings, to other people, and to how they react to us. Yet, so often these things have very little to do with us. We feel threatened because if something's wrong with our diversions then we must be alone with ourselves.

66

A number of High Point University students take the chapel services for a course credit under Religion 119. I mention them because at the end of the term they produce a short reflection paper on the services. One of the questions they write about concerns the most meaningful aspect of the chapel worship. I've now read over 600 of those papers and the hands-down winner as most often cited is this: "The chance to come to chapel and be quiet and pause for 45 minutes in the middle of the week and be alone and get in touch with myself through just sitting and reflecting." That pause to be alone is critical for all of us. It helps us to face the ultimate reality: our own personhood.

One of the most brilliant philosophers in the history of education in America was William James. He did as much for philosophy and psychology as any educator has ever done for his or her disciplines. If you go to Harvard, the tallest building on the campus is William James Hall, a multi-storied white edifice which houses the psychology department. I think we can say that William James was as brilliant as any professor you will ever meet in any university in your lifetime.

William James recommended to his classes that they attend chapel frequently. He said he did this because chapel is the one place where you can be really alone and see yourself as you can nowhere else.

For whatever reason people worship, force of habit, for the music, for the credit, to please parents or whatever, there is little in the other dimensions of life which deals with the mysterious and ministers to our inescapable loneliness.

If you can conceive of God opening God's own hands and showing them to you and saying, "Behold, I have tattooed your name on my palms," you've got power. You can have a high opinion of yourself in the midst of the stormiest of times. If your name is tattooed on God's palms, you can stand alone and become your own best friend. You do not have to live by illusion.

And if you can be a friend to yourself, you can be a friend to others. You will be freed from your diversions and be free to be yourself.

You can even be courageous. You can stand for something. You can take risks. You can speak up for others; you can stand against injustice. You cannot be threatened or defeated. You can even stand alone. "Behold," says the Lord God, "I have tattooed your name on my palms."

This ability to accept reality, with all of its limitations, enables the Christian to drop the illusion of having to live in a comfortable world. Even our religious experience does not need to be a diversion from the discomforts of life. In fact, the individual who seriously wrestles with an imperfect world can embrace a certain *metanoia* consistent with the Christian faith.

The Illusion Of Comfort

Sometimes it is best to be a little uncomfortable with ourselves and our world. As long as we are uncomfortable with certain inequities in our world there is at least a chance that we will make a move to do something about them. At all costs you and I, if we are to remain Christian, must keep alive a certain uncomfortable feeling within ourselves.

A person who did that for me early in life was a boy named P.J. Crowley. I met P.J. when I was fourteen years old. At that time I was a member of the Sunday School in a First Baptist Church in South Carolina. My family was a somewhat typical lower middle-class family. We did not have much in the way of material possessions but we were at the economic level of almost every other family in our part of town. Consequently we were comfortable with who we were and what we had.

My mother gave me a dollar bill every Sunday to put in the offering plate when it was passed in Sunday School. The old First Baptist Church was directly across the street from a drug store where you could purchase a milkshake for fifty cents. You got it. Every time they passed that offering plate in Sunday School, I proudly dropped in 50 cents. I was comfortable doing that. It was as much as the other kids put in and my mother never knew the difference. Nothing wrong with a little self-centeredness when a chocolate shake was at stake. Besides, the Lord got half of it.

Well, that fateful Sunday morning one of the adults in the church brought a new boy to class. It was P.J. Crowley. I'll never forget P.J. He had a huge smile on his face virtually all the time. He was happy and quiet. He was also poor. All the rest of us boys wore white shirts and ties. P.J. always wore a rolled-up striped shirt, frayed at the collar, and no tie. His shoes had holes in them and his pants wore patches. I remember vividly the scene as the plate passed from boy to boy and P.J. proudly fished down into his pocket and withdrew a handkerchief. He unfolded it and took out three pennies and put them in the plate. Then he proudly passed it to the next boy. P.J. Crowley did this every Sunday and I never saw him in the drug store. Those three pennies were all he had. P.J. made me uncomfortable. I can still visualize his face and it's been 34 years. I started putting my whole dollar in the plate.

Sometimes you and I can become so comfortable with our lives we can't understand why other people aren't as comfortable as we are. We insulate ourselves with layer after layer of protective padding until we become insensitive to the pain of others in our world. It happens all the time. Churches get comfortable with their kind of folks. They live by illusion instead of reality. A man gets too comfortable with his wife — she's always there, so after awhile he doesn't even see her as a person, just his wife. He lives with the illusion of a wife instead of the reality of a person. Our children get so comfortable they can't summon the motivation to work or accept responsibility anymore. Even businesses and universities grow comfortable with their successes, living by the illusion of their special status instead of with the reality of their hurting world.

Some people in my city can live their whole lives in the northwest quadrant of town, moving between their homes, the mall, and the country club.

George Bernard Shaw presented an interesting notion of what hell is like. Instead of the traditional notion that hell is a place of torment and torture, Shaw described it as *a place where comfortable people lose their sensitivity.*

An old woman boasts to Don Juan that she just knows she is not in hell. She assures him that since she feels no pain she can't be in hell. Don Juan assures her that this is the guarantee that she is indeed in hell. He replies, "Hell ... is a place for the wicked. The wicked are quite comfortable in it: it was made for them. You tell me you feel no pain. I conclude you are one of those for whom hell exists ... the truly damned are those who are happy in hell."[25]

Don Juan contrasts heaven as a place where you face things as they are.

I think this is perhaps a message our egocentric generation needs to hear. We can become too comfortable — too comfortable with our privileges, too comfortable with our limited knowledge, and too comfortable with our religion. I tell you an observation I have made — the worst preaching in the world is that which lets you leave church feeling comfortable.

Consider some of the images of the church which have become dominant in the mid-1990s. Some see the church as a "spiritual clinic." Just as smart businesses meet the felt needs of their customers, so do churches meet the needs of their customers. In such a clinic the pastor does spiritual diagnosis and counseling from the pulpit so that I "feel good" about myself and God when I leave church. The preacher "pumps me up" so I can meet the illusions of *my* world and I do not have to face the reality of the needs of others.

Another image of the church is that it is a normal shield for the community, somewhere between a good police department and fire department. It's a place where our children can be taught the faith and our family can be watched over when we are ill.

A final bogus image of the church is that it is a retreat from the pagan culture. Church becomes a place where my family and I can be insulated with other "good" people from this awful world. Thus insulated, I can take comfort that my children will grow up with the proper set of values and beliefs. We need to have fun and be with our friends. To minister to outsiders and welcome them would destroy our comfort zone, so let us embrace the idolatry of the family.

The basic premises of these images are flawed for all their elements of truth because they embrace only a partial vision. And they can all become much too comfortable.

70

You and I need all the discomfort our faith can inflict on us.
We need a few P.J. Crowleys, Malcolm Xs, Martin Luther Kings,
Mother Teresas, and the like to contend with. They may never be
our mentors but they are essential for us. Let us think of ourselves
as living in a house with several windows. At each window is a
different view. If we, out of comfort and habit, always go to the
same window and focus on the same buildings, the same trees,
and the same horizon, we overlook some things in our lives that
need attention. Our power in life exists in our ability to risk
occasionally becoming uncomfortable enough to change the focus
of our attention.[26]

In the light of this fact about life, Jesus speaks to us in Luke 16
a parable. It begins, "There was a rich man." The words haunt us
because it is a terrible thing if the only statement that can be made
about a person is that he was "rich." Imagine trying to express in
a single sentence that which is most characteristic of a person:
"He was a loyal friend. He was a good father. He was a civic
leader." But here is a case where you describe a man's whole life
by saying that he was very rich; he feasted like a glutton every
day, and he owned a magnificent wardrobe.[27]

People like this have to become absorbed in their wealth. They
have to insulate themselves in it, becoming comfortable associating
only with others who have it. So the rich man shut his eyes when
his carriage rode through the slums. He could not see Lazarus
with his sores and filthy rags living right next door. The rich man
had no one around him to make him uncomfortable enough to
notice Lazarus. His clothes, his food, his friends made him too
comfortable with his life. He became blind to his ultimate fate.

Do you realize there is no place in the Bible where the devil is
depicted as unattractive? Most of us do not fail when we are
struggling with our woes or wrestling with our problems or
swimming through a sea of red ink. We fail most often at being
human when we become too comfortable with our illusions. We
become insensitive to others in our world, sometimes even at our
own back door.

Why do we continue to live as we live? Well, it feels good!
It's comfortable. That chocolate milkshake tasted a whole lot better

than putting that dollar in the offering plate, I can tell you that. Why do people continue to smoke if they know smoking puts them at greater risk for lung cancer? Let me tell you that Salem cigarette tastes good and I feel comfortable with it. Why do people continue to live irresponsible lives, placing themselves at extreme risks for acquiring AIDS? Sex feels so good and everybody's doing it. Our society is comfortable with sexual irresponsibility. Why do the rich continue to destroy our society, our educational systems, and our children by their greed, their selfishness, and their blindness? It's not that people become manipulative and calloused on purpose. Humans just get too comfortable with the illusions in their surroundings. Here is where the Bible and our faith speak to us. Here is where the church *should* speak to us. It should make us profoundly *uncomfortable* with the inequities in life. If the church just makes us comfortable, it isn't helping us. You see, we can take our sins of blind comfort to a psychiatrist and the psychiatrist can help us become an adjusted sinner. We can take our sins of blind comfort to a physician and the physician can help us become a healthier sinner. We can make a great deal of money and become a wealthier sinner. But the church is supposed to trouble us, to make us uncomfortable with our ease, our lifestyles, and our blindness. If it does not do this and we become insensitive to the Lazarus figures in our world, then it has failed us miserably.

Gary Redding repeats a story of how comfort and enjoyment can become a deceptive power in our lives. One frigid day a great golden eagle spotted the carcass of an animal floating down the Niagara River. The eagle swooped down from his high perch and dug his talons into the body. He began to gorge himself on this newly discovered feast. As he ate, the alert eagle realized he was nearing the point where the water dropped over the falls. But he thought he was free to fly away whenever he wanted. He continued to eat. Finally, when the carcass reached the edge of the falls, the great eagle spread his wings to fly away. He could not budge. His feet were frozen to the carcass. He was taken over the edge to his death. He had become more and more comfortable as he ate and more and more captive to his eating.[28] He could not face the limits his reality set before him. In short, he had become so comfortable

72

with his illusion of eating his fill without personal consequences that he lost his fear of danger. He was no longer scared of his deadly situation.

Fear And Wisdom

All of us get scared. We fear those things in life which we perceive can hurt us. Bugs, roaches and crawly, creepy things hold no special allure for me. Only we humans can make a joyous occasion, like Halloween, out of our fears. And we adults can get caught up in the spirit of things as well. Only our generation could laugh at the crude and dangerous antics of two characters named Beavis and Butthead as they dance through harm's way buttressed by four-letter words and insolent behavioral patterns.

Fear is no laughing matter. The things that go bump in the night can indeed hurt us. They are part of our acceptance of reality. One of my favorite figures in the entertainment industry was Walt Disney. No one was better at creating meaningful children's movies than Walt Disney. Yet even Disney received complaints from many parents. You see, in every Walt Disney movie there came an episode when the world darkened, the music changed, and life became dangerous, frightening, and painful. Snow White actually swallowed the poisoned apple. Bambi's mother died. Old Yeller caught rabies and had to be shot. Cinderella's father died and she became a servant to her wicked stepmother in her own house. The one hundred and one dalmatian puppies were stolen in order to be killed and used for fur coats. Sleeping Beauty, under the curse of a witch, pricked her finger and slept for a hundred years.

Many parents protested to Disney that such things were not suitable to children's movies. Disney, however, refused to omit such episodes even though they frightened many children. He contended that any presentation of life is incomplete without such episodes. Whether we like it or not, life can hurt us, deeply and terribly. There is much to fear at any age.

In the kind of world we live in, people are taught to live in a hyper-vigilant manner. *New York Times* columnist Patricia Volk remembers her father telling her when she was six years old, "If a man attacks you, you knee him in the privates." She learned at an early age to walk in the center of the street, to tap a pencil on the mouthpiece of the phone when obscene callers called and say, "Yes, officer; it's him again," and not to put her purse in the grocery cart at the supermarket.[29]

I'm often amazed at how parents of prospective students size up a campus. The important ratio is not books per student but how many call boxes do you have (our university has seven) and how far apart are they? Campus safety is now the most often questioned issue by visiting parents. Our campus is secured with lights on timers, random patrols and walkie-talkies. We spend tens of thousands of dollars so students and faculty won't be afraid. And no matter what we do, it can never be enough. It seems to be our human condition both to be constantly wounded and to wound. As we live this dangerous adventure called life there is much both outside and within us that can destroy us.

We humans can be savage beasts. Nothing in nature is so well equipped for hurting or hating as a human being. Psalm 139:14 has the Psalmist saying these words to God: "I praise you because I am fearfully and wonderfully made." You and I are wonderfully made. But we are also fearfully made. We are made as free beings in whose hands much potential harm lies. Confuse and frighten us and we will lash out at anything. Crowd us and we will rob and destroy. Deprive us and we will retaliate. Impoverish us and we will burn down our own cities in the night. Excite us, frighten us, anger us in a crowd and we can become more devastating than swarms of locusts or herds of animals. Society, in the words of Carlyle Marney, can sometimes be "a composite picture of (our) great power to harm."[30]

I've been associated with campus ministry or churches near university campuses for 23 years. Currently I am privileged to teach an honors section of a religion course. It has thirteen honor students in it. But I have nineteen former students who are currently in prison as I speak to you. Those nineteen would be a great section, academically as bright and capable as any honors section. Their reasons for being in prison vary: one strangled her own baby, newly delivered in the residence hall shower, and hid it in a shoe box in her closet; one murdered his girlfriend with a shotgun; another robbed one of her city's pharmacies in broad daylight.

I know what humans can do to themselves and others. I have fear. One would be an idiot not to have some fear. That's reality.

But that fear is also the beginning of wisdom. That's why I teach. Given our nature, if we should suspend for a single ten years the processes of education, our great civilization would be in ruin. If we should destroy past our own generation's memory the knowledge of etiquette, laws, and patterns of civilized conduct, we would be glorified apes and swamp creatures again. That is our very real *fear*. More than occasionally professors are asked: "Why should I have to take a course in religion or a foreign language or behavioral sciences or English literature? I'm going to be an accountant. I'll never professionally use these courses."

No, few students *professionally* utilize most of the courses outside their major. I agree. Humans take those courses to help subdue their powers of destruction. Art, culture, philosophy, music, religion, history, psychology — all these and many more are needed to cage and tame the human strength for evil. Our fear of what we will be like if we do not learn about our potential for evil is what enables us to begin to develop wisdom. In a strange way, fear of yourself is actually the beginning of wisdom.

Our society talks a great deal about having what it calls an "informed conscience." If you analyze that statement it implies that a conscience is largely the result of information. People are always telling us that to make humans more moral we have only to offer more education. You have heard the argument: if you have access to more information about values and patterns of behavior then you will become a person of better and better conscience. The truth is, conscience by itself is never good. It is limited by factors of environment, upbringing, and personal character.

Herbert O'Driscoll is right: "Conscience needs grace."[31] Conscience must have a source of inspiration beyond the **self**. We must be so afraid of our evil that we find inspiration not just when we desire it, but when we need it, which is each and every week of our lives.

75

As we encounter those things that can destroy us we need to be afraid. We need to be afraid of our tendency to set ourselves up as our own god. We need to fear our own pride. We need to fear our wickedness, our lust, our deceit, our search for prestige and prominence and our own underhanded arrogance.

You see, our problem is often not what we fear in life but what we do *not* fear. When we cease to fear what we could become and consider ourselves more important than our creator, we have lost wisdom.

Our problems in life will not come from our sexuality.

Our problems will not come from our heredity or our environment.

Our problems will not be chemical or biological.

Our problems, if we are not careful, will come from our lack of wisdom: our inability to accept the reality of our limited existence.

Our churches are limited. All businesses are limited. We should never labor under the illusion that they are not. Yet at the same time, if we are to remain true to our Christian calling, we must live by grace and hope. Such will demand that we somehow, in our aloneness and imperfection, find pockets of existence which enable us to live beyond some of the limitations humans place upon our social institutions.

When The Public Is Not Cordially Invited

Advertising can be dangerous. This is especially true for churches. Each time I read an advertisement in the newspaper for a special event a church is holding, I tend to do a double-take when I see those italicized words at the bottom of the ad, "The Public Is Cordially Invited To Attend." I wonder what would happen if "the public" actually showed up? When I was student in seminary I served as summer youth director for a Baptist church in a little farming community. We were, by far, the largest church in town. Consequently most of the town's middle-class youth revolved their summer activities around that church.

76

As we planned a Sunday evening study group, I booked a film by Bill Cosby. The film dealt with current American youth values. Now, these were the days before Bill Cosby became the fashionable and popular Dr. Huxtable.

The minister of the church and I looked over the brochure and decided that such a fine program was just too good to keep a secret. "Run an ad in the paper," the minister suggested. "Put your picture in it, describe the film, and add 'The Public Is Cordially Invited To Attend.'" Well, we did just that and the little bi-weekly town newspaper ran the advertisement on the front page.

The night of the program a horrible thing happened: by golly, the *public* showed up! I mean the public showed up! The whole public showed up. We were all thrown together in sharply contrasting mixes. The gathering was about sixty percent white, thirty percent black, and ten percent Hispanic. The president of the gas company sat in his three-piece suit, surrounded by his two teenage daughters who attended the fine and exclusive private high school. Next to him sat another white man, one of the town's garbage collectors, dressed like he was getting ready to leap on the truck for the Monday morning run. He had his two teenage sons with him and they looked and smelled as if they had not taken a bath in five years.

The black woman who served as the high school guidance counselor was sitting there with a frown on her face next to a black man who served as night watchman at the local meat plant. The man smelled of alcohol and the counselor kept moving her chair away from him inch by inch.

An awful sense of estrangement and alienation descended immediately upon the room. The have-nots, the unfits, dominated the conversation that evening. But I could tell by the scowls on their faces that the other folks didn't feel much like talking anyway. They were reserving their words for the next day.

I doubt that my reputation ever recovered in their eyes. The rest of the summer was an uphill battle. The next day, the poor minister simply put his head on the desk and moaned, "I can't believe they showed up." Nothing like that had ever happened in that church. We, obviously, did not run anymore "The Public Is

Cordially Invited To Attend" advertisements. The public, of course, was not really invited in the first place. There is a great problem when uninvited people, especially misfits, come to something that is supposed to be "respectable."

Lest you laugh totally at the churches, consider the universities. We want our students to study self, society, and the world and to be knowledgeable in international studies. We want them prepared to meet the world upon graduating from here. Or do we? Do we really want them to meet the world? We have to have fences to protect ourselves from the public. We have "no trespassing" signs around our facilities and each week the security reports contain accounts of innumerable "townies" thrown out of the gymnasium. We all know the public will mob us, rob us, and mug us. We want and need to get SAT scores up so much of the public can't qualify for admission. And, being one who receives four university alumni magazines, I notice that no articles are ever written on unsuccessful graduates who are just part of the public. We want you to rise above the public. The incongruity of it all is perhaps not lost on the public.

Can't you identify with the poor Pharisee in the seventh chapter of Luke who gave the dinner party for Jesus? He was a respectable man, a professional minister. The party was held at noon and it was meant to be a private dinner. Simon had invited Jesus in the belief that Jesus was a prophet.

It was going to be a grand party. The scene must have been a striking one. Such a man as Simon strives for excellence. He was there smiling and acting as if he knew everyone, whether he did or not. The great prophet was coming. Several people had perhaps written their best questions to ask.

Despite the fact that it was meant to be a private dinner, many uninvited "townies," the public, gathered around the head banquet table. They were whispering among themselves, "Who is this? Who is this who even forgives sins?"

If that were not enough, in walked a woman from the streets. She had come all the way from uptown. She was a prostitute. Horror of horrors, she brought a flask of ointment. She stood behind Jesus, the invited guest, and she began to cry. Then she started sobbing and slobbering all over Him. She bent over and wiped His feet with the hair of her head. Then she began to kiss His feet. She was ruining the gala affair, the big party.

This scripture, given its setting, is an unbelievable story, isn't it? What a contrasting mix of characters. But *Jesus seems to always throw together people of sharp contrasts.* The story of the Pharisee and the sinful woman is not the only example. Among the poor, the lame, and the blind we find the rich young man. In the middle of the cultured traveler, the pious priest, and the lofty Levite, we find an untouchable Samaritan. The Pharisee and the publican both go up the hill to pray.

It does appear to be something less than excellence that Jesus used in His personal illustrations. And this has to be of significance to a world which, rightfully so, strives for excellence. Donald Nichols writes speeches for corporate executives.[32] He notes that in the past few years the gurus in the corner office began to covet a metaphor with which to adorn their efforts. They searched for an epigram, a shibboleth, a word to emblazon all they were about. The word appeared from two writers, Thomas Peters and Robert Watterman, who made their livelihood consorting with the pharaohs. The word was *excellence.* Soon we were knee-deep in corporate *excellence*, educational *excellence*, personal *excellence*. Religious writers began to focus on *The More Excellent Way.* Excellence came to be viewed as a principle to "stay on top of the heap." One of the favorite stories of Peters and Watterman was about a Honda worker who, on his way home each evening, straightened up windshield wiper blades on all the Hondas he passed. He just couldn't stand to see a flaw in a Honda.[33] That's excellence.

I think it correct to say that this excellent Pharisee, named Simon, dismissed Jesus as being a true prophet. "If this man were a prophet," said Simon, "He would have known what kind of woman is touching Him, for she is a sinner!" (Luke 7:39). In other words, *a true Son of God is a person who just can't stand to see a flaw in one of his products.* A true Son of God would be above the public.

Jesus uttered an absolutely ridiculous perspective — *the survival of the unfit public!* Those who feel they are forgiven for much tend to love more than those who feel they have little to be forgiven for. In a strange way, the Pharisee-host also had a sickness, a condition that needed forgiveness. Because everything had gone so well with him, he had never had much opportunity to learn to sympathize with others. He was so caught up in his own judgments that he could no longer find God in anyone who had what he considered to be a "flaw."

The biblical record announces with absolute clarity that it is not always the fittest who reach the Kingdom. If the unfit public does not survive, then we are all doomed. We are all a part of that unfit public. The apostle Paul tried to grasp and articulate the essence of Jesus' life in these words: "For *all* have sinned and come short of the glory of God" (Romans 3:23). "There is none righteous, no, not one" (Romans 3:10).

To return to my situation in a church-related university, one might ask, "What's the point in this?" We sit removed from the public with everyone somewhat leveled out — the same tuition costs, blacks and whites together, people from rich backgrounds and some from poor backgrounds, the same number of hours and core courses required for graduation. We sit here apart from the public for a period of time sequestered behind the fence — and within the university buildings — for what? Surely the public is not leveled out like this?

Actually, if only for four years, we are here to live in a way the public has not yet invented. We are here to get a little taste of what the Kingdom of God is like. Beethoven has always impressed me with his hope for what the future might hold. Do you know that *Beethoven wrote music that could only be properly played on instruments that his society had not yet invented?* That's hope in the future. We are called to live on our campus in ways that the public has not yet invented.

Perhaps Rabbi Abraham Herehel said it best in a parable he told. It seems that there was a kingdom in which, due to a horrible accident, the entire grain crop had been poisoned. Anyone who ate the grain became crazy. Because there were few other food supplies available the people were faced with a tragic choice: eat the grain and go crazy or not eat the grain and starve to death. The king surveyed the situation and came to a conclusion. "Very well," said the king, "let us eat the grain, for we cannot starve to death. But let us at the same time pull aside a few people and feed them a different diet, so we will always have a group around us who will know that we are crazy and can tell us so."

The college experience, for whatever else it is worth, is a time to eat a different diet, if only for four years. It's a time to worship ecumenically, to study great universal truths, to embrace all manner of diversity and common guests. It's a time and place to eat a different diet from what we may have to eat in the rest of society. It's a time to learn that it is not always the fittest who reach the kingdom. It's a time to reflect on this before getting out into the world with its particularity, its status and monetary divisions, and its thirst for wealth. It's a time to eat a diet that will one day help us remember that the world is crazy. It's a time for discovering our common humanity.

When John had his wonderful revelation on Patmos, he saw two crowds entering into the Kingdom of God. The first crowd was the 144,000 — the chosen nation, the advantaged, the expected crowd — the fittest 144,000 who made it. Now, that's sobering. Think of all the people who have ever lived and will ever live on the face of our planet. Greensboro has more than 144,000 people. That's a tiny crowd. This first crowd was recognized and named: Benjamin, Reuben, and so on.[34] Those are, indeed, the fittest. And they made it!

That's scary. I don't want to be locked out of the Kingdom of God. 144,000! Of all the people who ever lived! I'm not in the top 144,000! I guarantee you, Hal Warlick probably isn't in the top 144 million people who ever lived. We may not have anyone in our university in the top 144 million. When you consider all who have ever lived, the fittest 144,000 is preposterous. We're doomed. We are doomed.

Ah, but wait. John also saw a second crowd behind the first crowd. He saw *a nameless host*, the unfit public, coming along behind. Some were crippled. Some were wounded. Some were crawling and some were bleeding. Some were broken. Some were scattered. Some were scarred.

Who are these? Who are these? I want to know! I want to know! These are the unfit. These are they who are dead but now they live. These are they who have been forgiven. These are they for whom the Lamb died. These are they for whom the blood was shed. This is the public that is cordially invited to enter the Kingdom of God.

The entire message of the gospel comes down to one earthshaking vision, one eternal scene that shivers its way out of the cold corridors of doom — John saw *two* crowds entering the Kingdom — the fit few and the unfit public! It is enough to make you want to run outside and scream, isn't it? The public, of which we are a part, is cordially invited into God's Kingdom. That, too, is a reality with which we can live. So powerful is this reality that it can give us the courage to redraw our relational landscape as we honestly wrestle with our all-too-human limitations.

Chapter Four

Redrawing The Landscape

One summer's day my wife and I journeyed to Pittsburgh, Pennsylvania, to attend a conference. We packed early in the morning and joined a colleague and his wife for breakfast. The other couple was also attending the Pittsburgh conference. After saying "goodbye" to our friends, we indicated that we would see them at the hotel in Pittsburgh. We were leaving directly from the breakfast while they were not leaving for another two or three hours, after they went home, packed, and took their children to the hotel. Diane and I pounded up to Pittsburgh, driving a few miles over the speed limit and stopping only for gas. When we arrived at the hotel, we carried our luggage from the car, and there to our amazement was the other couple by the swimming pool. "Where have you been?" he asked. "We've been here over an hour."

"You must have flown up here! How fast were you going?" I retorted.

"Fifty-five miles an hour," he said.

"Well," I began. "I came the best way the map showed."

"Let me see that map," he stated, grabbing it from my hand.

"This thing is three years old. They've opened up a new interstate to Pittsburgh."

Boy, was I miffed. That old map cost me nearly two hours of extra driving.

New maps are a necessity in today's world. Consider this: a person who follows a two-year-old map of North Carolina no longer knows the way to get to Wilmington. He or she would travel an hour out of the way getting to the beach, since I-40 is now open.

You and I live our lives according to the maps we have drawn for ourselves in terms of what the world is really like. We began making these maps when we were little children. If we are wise and committed to the journey of life, we will continue to work on these maps all our lives.

Dr. Scott Peck has written a book called *The Road Less Traveled*. In it he talks about the ability to see the world as it really is as a necessity for wholeness. All of us, says Peck, live off our own maps of reality, our imagined perception of the world as it really is.

A major problem in life is when people do not upgrade their maps of reality. Sometimes when we are adults, we find ourselves still trying to operate with the maps we drew when we were small children. Consequently, we can go through life not truly understanding the reality of the adult world we live in, much less the reality of God's goodness.

Psychologists have a definition for people who try to live in their adult world with the maps they drew as children. The definition is *transference*. It is a way of seeing the world through a map that was developed in childhood and was entirely appropriate to childhood but which is inappropriately transferred into adult situations. The apostle Paul spoke vividly of the acceptance of reality when he told the Corinthians: "When I was a child, I spoke like a child, I thought like a child, I reasoned like a child; when I became an adult, I gave up childish ways ..." (1 Corinthians 13:11).

Let me illustrate this phenomenon. I'm certain that your parents at times unconsciously disappointed you or let you down when you were a child. Occasionally all parents are guilty of this. Perhaps they promised you a trip for your birthday and then forgot about it and gave you a sweater instead. It happens all the time. That's normal. But if it happens too often and disappointment follows disappointment, the child depicts lack of caring and learns not to trust them. Then, in his childish way, he forms his map of reality on the basis of this repeated experience. *It diminishes a person's pain to believe other persons are basically untrustworthy*; that way they don't have to expect anything. A child psychologist once told me, "Always follow through on your promises to children; otherwise, don't promise. You have to be consistent. Don't say you're going to do something and then not follow through." You see, from the realization that "I can't trust my parents" the child can conclude "I can't trust anybody." And real disaster occurs when this map which serves fine in childhood is carried into the adult world. Then, if you do not bother to test that map to see if other people are truly untrustworthy, you develop and expect the worst. It is a syndrome which affects how you deal with everybody who is important in your life — your girlfriend or boyfriend, your spouse, your employers, your church, your government, and on and on. Many of us can become angry with life and quarrel with it on the basis of a map of reality drawn when we were little boys or little girls. We can become unaware of the positive aspects of reality.

One of the paramount awarenesses made by Jesus Christ and the apostle Paul was that human beings don't like to change their maps once they have drawn them. Even when our life maps aren't working well for us, we don't like to change them. It's shaky business redrawing your map. But *if you don't redraw an inadequate map, you're not living in reality.* If, for example, you are still using your childhood religion as the only map to get through adulthood, you may be more off-line than you think. And if you are still treating people the same way and expecting the same things from them as you did when you were a child, you may be headed in the wrong direction. Perhaps you know how this works. When I was in college, my best friend received a birthday gift every year on December 18th from his aunt in Hattiesburg, Mississippi. He hadn't seen her in years. The gift was always for a twelve-year-old boy. My friend would laugh and say, "Aunt Grace still thinks of me as a little boy." Frankly, I imagine that many of us stormed out of our homes sometime during many a Christmas holiday saying, "Mamma, I'm not twelve any more." Both my parents are dead now, I'm sorry to say, but even when they came to visit me in my 30s I was in some respects still their sixteen-year-old Harold, Jr., according to the map they were going by in trying to understand me. At times it was frustrating.

Much of the societal frustration and personal anger which assaults contemporary Americans eventuates from the inability of individuals to redraw their inherited maps from the 1960s. We

85

bring forth the realities of the past and become angry when we view a world which appears to exhibit a declining condition for us all. To be certain, our problems have greatly changed. The top problems in America's public schools in 1940 were identified by teachers as the following: "talking out of turn, chewing gum, making noise, running in halls, cutting in line, dress code infractions, and littering." When teachers were asked in 1990 to identify the top problems in public schools they pointed out: "drug abuse, alcohol abuse, pregnancy, suicide, rape, robbery, and assault."[35]

In like manner, the change in cultural indicators from the previous generation to the present indicates a drastically changed landscape. According to the U.S. Department of Justice, eight out of every ten Americans will be a victim of violent crime at least once in their lives. Violent crimes rose from 188 per 10,000 persons in 1960 to 589 per 10,000 persons in 1991 and the statistic keeps leaping.

The family structure has helped contribute to poverty. Single-parent homes are the order of the day as we move toward the twenty-first century. In 1960 only 2.3 percent of all births were to unmarried women. By 1990, 21 percent of all births were to unmarried women.[36] The number of divorces has increased in America by almost 200 percent in the last thirty years, which greatly exacerbates our problems. In his incisive book, *Poor Support: Poverty in the American Family*, David T. Ellwood points out that 73 percent of children from single-parent families will be in poverty at some point in their childhood.[37] The realities are certainly enough to frustrate and even anger the most dedicated Christian. How do we respond at the personal level? Do we simply accommodate the cultural realities or do we have to summon new resources and perspectives for new conditions?

When he was eight years old, I took my oldest son to a store in Massachusetts to buy him his very first baseball glove. I let him pick it out and we made a big deal over it. We even pitched ball in the aisle to make certain it was the right one. Maybe he'll remember it and maybe he won't. But for years I had remembered how I got my first glove. My mother had saved Green Stamps to buy the glove. I didn't know that at the time. When I was growing up, grocery stores gave stamps to the customers based on the dollar amounts purchased. You pasted these S & H Green Stamps in little coupon books. Then you could go to a stamp redemption center and trade your books of stamps for prizes. It took years to fill up the books. You could trade ten books for a toaster. Of course, you had to purchase groceries for a year to get enough for the toaster. But many homemakers were into that — getting something extra for nothing. And occasionally, you could get something after a few years that you didn't have the extra money to purchase as a luxury.

On my thirteenth birthday, I walked into the house, having asked for a baseball glove for months. Mother couldn't be home, so she left my present on the table. There it was in a brown S & H Green Stamp bag — a baseball glove. It was horrible. My folks knew nothing about baseball. It was too small. It was too inflexible. It was too cheaply made. I never used it a single time. I told my mother I did not like it. I wound up purchasing a used glove from a friend for $5.00. After many months, I threw the Green Stamp glove in the trash, still brand-new and unused.

From that and several other legitimate experiences I carried certain memories into a road map for life for a long time — my parents were poor, uninformed, and very much people who had to struggle against life. I had the road map of a victim. It angered me.

Then, many years later, immediately before the funeral service for my mother, Bob, my hometown friend and college roommate, walked over. He said, "Warlick, you certainly were lucky. Your mother had a wonderful life and was so privileged in many ways." I responded, "Are you kidding me? She had to struggle like crazy. My first baseball glove came from Green Stamps and we almost went bankrupt twice." Bob quickly answered. "No, that's not what I meant. Look over at the casket at Randy, Ward, Johnny, and Jimmy. And at me. Your mother taught us all and influenced our lives in Sunday School and Cub Scouts. Not many women have ever helped raise two Rhodes scholars and the chiefs of staff of two university hospitals." And I remembered that on the day of my first baseball glove, mother had been at an all-day teacher's workshop at the church. And during the year of the Green Stamps, our church had built a new building and we had gotten a little over-involved in it. *Mother got the glove wrong but she got life right.* Gloves are important to children, much more so than values. But adults ought to know better and should redraw that map to deal with the reality of the adult world. If not, *we'll always get the glove right but get life wrong* and place on ourselves perceived limitations that may not exist.

We lose touch with reality when we do not redraw our maps for living on the basis of new information. One of the constant themes in the New Testament is that Jesus is the Way, the Truth and the Life, and that in Him we become new creatures following a new map.

One day when His mother and brothers came seeking Him, Jesus left them standing long enough to say this to His followers: "My real mother and brothers and sisters are those who do the will of God." Now Jesus was not rejecting His family. Nor was He rejecting family values. He was simply drawing a new map of reality. He was insisting that there is a reality beyond the earthly family, an allegiance beside which even family ties must take second place. There is an even greater family to which we belong. Being baptized by the Holy Spirit into the Kingdom of God causes you to understand reality in a new way. We have to redraw our personal maps on the basis of the family of God to which we belong. *One* family of God. "By His spirit," says Paul, we have a new map. "We are all baptized into one body — Jew or Greek, slave or free — and all were made to drink of one Spirit." In baptism we are stamped as the property of God. This gives us a bond with one another that creates a manner of loving and being loved that turns life in another direction.

Only by turning to a reality which lies beyond the earthly family can we properly reappraise some of the threatening situations which confront our twenty-first century world. As we architect our souls for a new century, we must not enfeeble our perceptions or abandon our personal theological tasks. Many are they who can quote the morbid negative social indicators mentioned above. But there is other data to consider. In 1991 the divorce rate had dropped to its lowest point since 1979 (National Center for Health Services). In addition, by 1991 the number of children directly affected by divorce in America dropped to its lowest number since 1970. And while it sometimes seems fashionable to bash the young, consider this: according to the U.S. Department of Education, while in 1960 39 percent of our youth dropped out of high school, by 1990 the high school dropout rate had declined to only twelve percent. Indeed, by 1991 ninety percent of young Americans sixteen to 24 years old had completed high school. In its effort to provide every child with a high school education, the United States has far surpassed the more elite educational systems in Europe and Japan. When we consider that our youth have accomplished this in the face of aforementioned divorce, single-parent family and poverty ratios, we have to acknowledge something inspiring and courageous about that American spirit. In focusing on the problems, which admittedly are significant, we must not focus on the "glove" and get life wrong. Perhaps it is time for us to redraw our personal theological maps and deal with our anger, our relationships, our need for forgiveness, and our personal lifestyles.

Capping The Inner Volcano

It is not easy to be forgiving and kind in our kind of world. We all need space, and it is becoming harder to find. Our grandparents had lots of room. Agriculture was the primary method by which people earned a living. They could do pretty well as they pleased on their property. Heck, they did not even have to lock the doors. When you got mad at my Uncle Jack's farm, Mother just ran you outside to walk through the tobacco or corn fields until you cooled off. You didn't have to worry about being hit by a car or having someone try to kidnap you or sell drugs to you. Then, when you had cooled off, grandparents, parents, cousins, aunts and uncles, living in fairly close proximity, gave you a wide area over which to spread your feelings.

Our world is a lot more close up. We live house to house, apartment to apartment, town house to town house, room to room, suite to suite. We drive fender to fender. We work elbow to elbow.

And students at my university go to a small enough school to enable us to know almost everybody eventually. We often get in each other's way. And when we try to spread out our feelings, we often find that the larger family is no longer there to absorb them. We have to focus our anger on fewer people. It naturally becomes more intense.

Living close up has problems. We all love and hate the very people with whom we are the closest. The two feelings exist side-by-side.[38] Seventy percent admitted to emergency rooms in hospitals on Saturday night are victims of either domestic violence or violence among friends. All of us compete with one another for honors and recognition, and if we do not get them we become angry. We compete for power, and if we do not acquire it, more anger is generated. Fathers and sons compete with one another, and daughters and mothers compete with each other. We live in a competitive democracy.

And should people my age tend to get smug and say "we're past that state," let me also turn our hair on end: five hundred thousand to one million elderly are abused in this country every year. The most severe cases of violence seen by the family violence professionals have been unmerciful assaults on the elderly. And none of us is getting any younger. In fact, by the twenty-first century, the elderly will be the majority of the population in America.

What do we do when we are mad? Obviously we cannot eliminate anger from life. Nor should we. Differences between people don't just go away. If we don't express them, they fester. It isn't possible to be close to someone without being angry at times. We let our loved ones get close to us by letting them feel our anger when it is there. And if we get to the point where we are always caving in and valuing submission to others, then we will always be sad.

So how do we keep from being either sad or angry all the time?

Consider Jesus. Like most of us, he found it easier to be a star other places than in His own hometown. And He found it easier to accomplish great physical and medical feats than to remove anger from His own closest friends. Here was a man, the son of God, who could calm an entire sea in the middle of a raging storm and tell a leper he was healed. Yet, as Matthew's twentieth chapter indicates, He could not prohibit a jealous woman from making an idiotic statement or keep the other ten disciples from getting angry at her two boys. That's life, isn't it? We can often run a business or recover from surgery or complete a great service project or make the dean's list easier than we can dissipate our feelings of anger toward those closest to us.

Consequently, the person who cannot cope with anger in close-up relationships is going to be a pretty alienated person in our kind of world. "One of the very difficult tasks in growing up is that of accepting that we are not the axis around which everyone and everything revolves, that there are other people who are interested in themselves and are not particularly interested in us."[39]

We get angry when we feel helpless. We get caught in some bureaucratic system that we feel helpless to influence and we lash out before we get gobbled up. We get angry when we feel we are being neglected or ignored.

What happens to us when we get angry? Hate pumps up our blood pressure. More sugar pours into our system. The heart beats faster. More adrenalin is secreted to dilate the pupils of the eyes, and chemical changes occur in the blood. Even tissue changes take place. In fact, a good optometrist will not examine the eyes of an angry person. You see, anger distorts the retina through abnormal blood flow. Consequently, it is correct to say that a person who is angry most of the time is a sick person.

Jesus and the scriptures were interested in the health of human beings. That is why they talked about anger so much. When Jesus admonished His followers, "Bless them that curse you, pray for them that despitefully use you and persecute you," He wasn't trying to be "far out" or overly dramatic. You see, He was not making the statement for the benefit of others but for our own benefit. In order to be free and healthy, we must pray for those who we think are our enemies. We must channel those emotions into something positive, or like a rattlesnake we will bite ourselves to pieces when cornered. Anger is a form of energy. We can say "forget it." But no one can do that. Energy cannot be destroyed. It can only be converted into another form of energy.

Secondly, we must recognize that we love and hate those people who are closest to us. Consequently, *we must never cut ourselves off from those who get in our way and make us mad, or we will miss some of life's greatest blessings.* Look at Jesus, for example. Jesus got angry most often at His close disciples. He screamed at Peter and called him "a devil." He became irritated at the whole lot of them at Gethsemane when they all went to sleep on Him and then offered the excuse of being tired. He had to keep ten of them from punching out James and John and probably their mother, also. Compare His great calmness and compassion with outsiders — those whom He healed and forgave. Yet whom did Jesus return to after His resurrection? Not the crowd He fed with fish and bread. Not the woman with the bleeding ulcer or the man with the lame foot. He came back to that bunch of people that He argued with. And who were the people who gave their lives in faith to Jesus? Who wrote the gospels? *There is not a single gospel written by someone Jesus did not get angry at.* Not a single healed person wrote a gospel. Not a single person among the 5,000 on the hillside who witnessed the miracle of the loaves and fishes wrote a gospel. No cleansed leper or healed Samaritan stepped forward to write a gospel, did they? Those who followed and loved Jesus were the ones who lived close up with him; and those were the ones He occasionally became angry with.

So much of our fear and consequently our anger comes from self-pity. A family member has made it big and we haven't. Someone with not nearly as much talent as we have has gotten a lucky break and left us in the dust.

Few activities in life are more debilitating and more responsible for resentment and anger than self-pity. I know that about which I write. Self-pity is a special temptation to all people who give themselves to people, like parents, teachers, preachers, musicians, and social workers. We cry, "My time is never my own. I'm underpaid. I'm never appreciated. I never have time to do the things I want to do. People take advantage of me."

If you plan to be a leader in our society, I give you a huge piece of advice: learn now to deal with self-pity. Those who have heavy responsibilities laid on them, and all leaders do, are more prone to self-pity and anger than are others.

Believe it or not, those who are mad because of self-pity form a familiar mood in the Bible. We find a lack of appreciation firing the flames of anger everywhere. Namaan is angry and resentful because Mordecai has snubbed him. Elijah is sitting under a juniper tree feeling angry and sorry for himself. The Psalmist is writing about how mad he is over the fact that bad people are prospering in the world. He cries in Psalm 73: "The ungodly people increase in riches. I'm mad. I've cleansed my heart for nothing." And the classic view of a lack of appreciation is uttered by an elder brother to his father. "Look, Father, I'm mad. All these many years I've served you, done what you wanted, been home on time, never asked for much money, never broke the rules: yet you never gave *me* anything. But as soon as *my brother* came home, this one who broke every rule in the book, you have killed for him the fatted calf and thrown a party. I'm mad."

There appears to be much to be angry about in a world which constantly demands that we redraw our personal maps. Limits are hard to swallow. The old terrain of Protestant, Catholic, and Jew has been altered by the influx of Asian religions. We fear our children will not have the secure communities of faith that dotted our landscape. Women in the workplace resist, as they should, every effort to return to a pre-feminist perspective. White males fear having to turn over their hopes of getting a meaningful job to the dictates of the EEOC. Now the men's movement has grown in numbers to stand side-by-side with the women's movement, both claiming discrimination. And they're both pretty angry about it.

I suggest that the place to begin is in learning to face our fears. If anger comes primarily from fear, then it's our fear we have to deal with. My friend Frederick Buechner[40] says that the unwritten law of many families, including the one he grew up in, is this: Don't talk, don't trust, don't feel. Don't talk! Don't trust! Don't feel! In fact, I believe this law somehow gets translated to education and the workplace. Keep your mouth shut (play your hurts close to the vest); don't let the people you are with know your weaknesses. Don't trust (never turn your back on anybody). Don't feel; that way you won't get hurt.

We pay a huge price for not talking, not trusting, and not feeling. We never develop the giving, loving side of what we might have been as human beings. And that's where much of our suffering comes from.

I can understand the refusal to admit one's fears. When I grew up there were lots of messages about what you should do in order to be a real man:

Join the fraternity.
Play sports.
Get it on with lots of girls.
Be tough; fight if anybody insults you.
Stand your ground.
Drink lots of beer.
Get a good job, work hard, and be wealthy.
Be popular.

Talk about fear. We lived under the dread of being labeled a weakling, a queer, a wimp, or a sissy.

But I'm not certain my generation is any less scared than this generation. Most of us think, "If I tell the innermost things about myself, I will be rejected or put down." Isn't that still a genuine fear? Don't talk, don't trust, don't feel.

Men get scared. We live with a conquering mentality. The central metaphor that dominates most of our male world of conquest and competition is power. Look at the way we define ourselves: muscle power, sexual power, financial power, personal power, political power, the power of knowledge, and even the power of positive thinking.[41] No wonder we have a hard time separating aggression and anger. And women, God bless them, are proving no different as they enter the arenas where competition and conquest are honored. Now women's fear and anger enable them to have the same disease profile and early death as men.

What a world. We struggle to fulfill a thousand impossible expectations — I'm supposed to be competitive but gentle; I'm supposed to be ruthless and get things done at the office but tender toward my wife and children; I'm supposed to be efficient but

94

sensual and sexy, to take care of the opposite sex but treat them as equals. And so are you. Small wonder we are angry or sad. And when we get angry or sad we take it out on the young ones or the old folks. We resort to anger and violence because we feel impotent and scared.

Fortunately, our Bible is also a record of how people through the centuries have resolved anger. I turn our attention to the story of Joseph. I like this story because it goes against much of what I fear. It's a story of what happens in life when people tell the innermost things about themselves. Instead of being rejected or put down, Joseph's brothers find just the opposite happening. It's a story of forgetting and forgiving and lowering barriers between people.

You perhaps know the story of the life of Joseph. His brothers despised him. He was daddy's favorite. Daddy bought him a coat of many colors. He tattled on his brothers, got out of all the tough work around the house, and was always dreaming of owning the whole world. Finally, the brothers had had enough. They threw him into a pit, sold him into slavery in Egypt and told their daddy that he'd met with an unfortunate accident.

But somehow in Egypt God raised Joseph up. He was maligned and abused, but God raised him up. He was in prison, but God raised him up. He became secretary of agriculture. He was in charge of the food in Egypt when the rest of the Middle East was experiencing a famine.

Lo and behold, the brothers of Joseph are sent into Egypt begging for food. They have to come before this very brother they had despised. And Joseph — well, he had the upper hand. They did not recognize him. What an opportunity for him to harbor anger over the past wrongs. Successful Joseph, living in Egypt, successful in his job, speaking like an Egyptian, acting like an Egyptian — a real chance to control, to conquer, to let his faith fade and his fear control. What a chance to salvage some self-esteem. Don't talk. Don't trust. Don't feel. It didn't happen that way.

Instead, Joseph wept so loudly that the Egyptians heard him and Pharaoh's household heard about it. He said, "I am Joseph!

... Come close to me. Don't punish yourself. Your father is my father. Your God is my God."

Later in the story the brothers' father, Jacob, died. The brothers were really fearful now: "Daddy's dead and he was the only thing that kept Joseph from us. Now Joseph can have his revenge." What to do? Don't talk. Don't trust. Don't feel. Stand your ground. We'd rather die than say we were wrong. We'd rather lose a leg than admit our ignorance and lose some of our pride. Don't talk. Don't trust. Don't feel. Be mad or sad. It didn't happen that way.

The brothers sent a letter: "Forgive your brothers the sins and wrongs they committed." Then they came down and threw themselves before Joseph. "We made a mistake and we'll be your slaves," they said.

Joseph responded, "I am not in the place of God. I did not make you. I am not your judge and jury. I'm not in the place of God."

This story is a story for the new century. It speaks volumes to us as we seek to redraw traditional boundaries and live within the limits of our humanity. We are one another's brothers and sisters. Your God is my God. Their God is our God. We are not the judge and jury of one another, regardless of the times and conditions in which we find ourselves. If we are to live at peace in these days we must learn to talk, trust, feel, and forgive. As we rub shoulders with Eastern religions, wrestle with new structures for the American family, and confront a shrinking piece of the global economy, perhaps the most vital of these traits for the Christian will be that of forgiveness. After all, that is what we are supposed to do best.

Perhaps governments, private enterprises, men's groups, women's groups, gay and lesbian caucuses, and media enterprises will help us reorder some of our patterns and responses to our ills. Yet forgiveness remains the sole charge to the Christian. It is this contribution of Christian people everywhere which holds forth the promise of a truly enjoyable life.

The Necessity Of Forgiveness

All across our political landscape new maps are being proposed: free trade agreements, health care reform, and educational mandates. Yet these efforts, by themselves, do not strike at the core of a reordered soul.

People who do not learn how to forgive do not enjoy life. The world hands us many irritating people. Some of them frustrate us to no end. If we embrace resentment instead of forgiveness, our relationships and our careers don't get very far. If you want to be a success in the world — major in forgiveness.

A newspaper carried the story of a man who bought a new Cadillac. Every time the car hit a slight bump there was an awful thumping. Twice he took the car to be examined. But they never could find the cause. Always there was the thumping. Finally, the servicemen narrowed the problem to one door of the car. When they took the door apart, they found a Coke bottle inside. In the bottle was a note which read: "So you finally found me, you wealthy ___ ___ ___ ___ (blankety-blank)." You see, a worker was so filled with resentment he thought he could destroy the satisfaction of the person who had enough money to buy a Cadillac. Actually, the worker's grudges and resentments had infested his own mind and his everyday job. The satisfaction being destroyed was his own.[42] Thus he made his work-life a slave to his perceived enemies. Our greatest danger in resentment lies not in the wrong done to us but in the wrong we can do to ourselves if we let ourselves become inwardly hardened. Can you imagine having to work in a job which stirs up a vindictive response in you? Who has the reward? You or your enemy?

How impossible Jesus' ideal seems at first — "Love your enemies and pray for them that persecute you." But on second glance it seems to be the most practical and rational rule for daily living that could be laid down. The only rewards in life come through working through relationships. There is no reward in having a *small* circle of like-minded friends.

Doris Donnelly, in her incisive book *Learning to Forgive*,[43] tells about a family she knew. They were very proficient in the use of resentment. They couldn't forgive anyone; nothing was

97

ever their fault. The family consisted of two parents and their three daughters. The friends of each family member were under constant scrutiny to determine whether or not they belonged to their group. The family socialized together, sat together in church, and participated in the community, all as a small group. Failing to include the three sisters in a birthday celebration, or not greeting a member of the group with beaming smiles and deferential courtesy, resulted in ostracism. *The family lived to be stroked by others.* It was as if the world owed them a stroking. One year the parents gave the same Christmas gift to each of the daughters' teachers, to the pastor of the church, and to the principal of the school. Anyone who did not respond immediately with profuse gratitude was eliminated from the list for the next time. The family took every delay as a personal slap in the face. And everyone scissored out of their lives knew there was little hope of being sewn into their lives again.

The mother of the family died suddenly. The father and the daughters naturally expected large crowds to gather for the final farewells. They enlisted the aid of the local police to handle traffic on the morning of the funeral. Phone calls were made to neighbors and to their "friends." Announcements were sent via telegram to people who had moved away. The local motels were alerted to save a few rooms for out-of-town guests who might appear at the last minute and need accommodations. Exactly ten people showed up for the funeral. The husband, the daughters, their husbands, one grandchild, and two members of their small circle of friends attended the services. It was truly embarrassing. The town laughed about it for years afterward.

People who scissor others from relationships think they are cutting people out of their lives. In reality they are cutting themselves out of the larger human family. They not only die alone, but whether they know it or not, they live alone as well.

As we live in our day and time, many trespasses will come against us. The world of the twenty-first century, with its limits and imperfections, can hurt us, as men and women have always been hurt. But it is our time, with our people, in our world. It is the only world we will have. It provides the only connection with life we can make.

It is a fact of existence that small circles of mutual resentments are not easily broken. You can take a group of goldfish that have been swimming for their lifetime in a small fishbowl out to the lake. You can turn them loose in the lake, but they will continue to swim in small circles, the dimension of their former bowl, for quite a while without accepting the massive freedom awaiting them. In terms of human behavior, Jesus called the phenomenon "saluting only your brethren." And He told it straight — "what reward is there in that?" It creates an attitude of smallness which is destructive to career, family, and self.

During the ministry in the villages of Galilee, Jesus preached passionately about forgiveness. It was a strange doctrine to most of the disciples. Peter wanted to be legal and statistical about it. But Jesus stated there is no limit to forgiveness. It's a matter of forgiveness becoming a part of the habit of your life. You can't forgive people 490 times without it becoming a permanent attitude. You cannot serve two masters. Either you will bow before the altar of revenge and scissor people out of your life, or you will bow before the altar of forgiveness and sew yourself into the wide fabric of humanity, as imperfect and impulsive as it is.

Peter had not realized the greatness of forgiveness. You cannot forgive people and pray for them, even if they persecute you, without becoming a person of love. Forgiveness creates a loving spirit. Jesus told Peter, "You must forgive from your heart." The key word is *kardia,* which is translated "heart." But the Greek word means more than the organ of the body. It means the seat of the inner person. Forgiveness is more than an act we do; it is an expression of who we are.

What an incredible power forgiveness turns loose. It is an expansive spirit. A person who has done his or her best and seen others walk off with what he wanted, who has planned and missed, aspired and failed, but can still walk through life with an unenvious and forgiving heart, being happy in his/her own best self, is a person who has won a great victory. *That person is a slave to no one. Life itself becomes his or her ally instead of enemy.*

The central thesis in Jesus's assertion about the kingdom of God was that small circles of people would become increasingly larger circles of people through winning over and including their perceived enemies. That is the acid test of Christianity. *Virtually every other group in society can do everything else Christians can do.*

Christians have programs. So does every other group. Christians celebrate Christmas. One group celebrates Shakespeare's birthday. Every social club celebrates its founder. Christians recite creeds — so do sororities, fraternities, and a thousand other groups. Christians sing songs. So does every group, from "ninety-nine bottles of beer on the wall" to "The National Anthem." Christians raise money. So does everyone else.

We are revealed as Christians only by the way we forgive other people, especially our enemies.

The greatness of Christianity lies not in its development of small pockets of congenial intimacies. The greatness of Christianity is in its expansive spirit that overthrows resentments, takes in enemies, embraces rivals and seeks the good in all sorts of people across all barriers that class and race can erect.

In our kind of world forgiveness is such a healthy ingredient. We do not live in a world that is politically correct. People become angry and resentful. You and I sometimes express negative feelings loudly and in public. Occasionally this has to be done. If we make people always feel guilty about expressing their less socially acceptable emotions, they will repress them. Later those emotions will often resurface as depression, anxiety, or rebellion. And we find ourselves on the outside looking in, when the more service-oriented world of the future rewards relationships more than manufacturing.

A Lifestyle For 2000

One of the interesting aspects of education would be quite humorous if it were not so tragic. Here are so many people trying to gain the credentials to get a good job, keep a good job, and improve in a job. We put our heads and minds in focus and try to

100

independently get our best grades. To work with others in the midst of a test would be cheating. To copy the work of another would be plagiarism at best and stealing at worst.

Yet the irony of the situation is this. Regardless of your credentials, your life will rise or fall depending on how you get along with other people. Three weeks after you have been on a job, no one cares where you went to school. The issue is: How well do you relate? One week I helped a physician move to Charlotte and a lawyer move back to Kernersville, North Carolina. They are great professionals, fine practitioners, and have degrees from superb universities. But their practices have gone up in smoke. They just can't get along with their partners.

In like manner, three years after you have been married, your spouse will not care much about the good times you used to have in college. He or she will rise with you or fall away from you depending on how you relate or don't relate in that marriage.

Given the stresses and strains incumbent upon us with the demands of twenty-first century living, relationships will assume a heightened importance. While it may seem strange, a clue to effective living in the future may well lie in the biblical witness. This witness emerges from a period in history when relationships were more important than programs and manufacturing. It illuminates our own search for theological meaning. As its pages unfold, we glean how people have tried to merge with other people, taken them over, or been taken over by others. David, for example, was a great king but a manipulative and lousy lover who committed murder because he wanted a relationship with a certain woman. Abigail, with very few options, wound up married to a drunkard. Kings and queens, saints and sinners seemed to fail at relationships. Great administrators were brought low, popular figures wound up on the garbage heap, and powerful physiques were rendered useless because they could not meet others as separate persons and find some peace in their relationships.

Perhaps no greater example need be stated than the one the Bible called Samson. He was strong and powerful. Women and girls were mesmerized by his good looks. Men and boys envied his sense of adventure and his strength. He had everything going for him. But everyone knew his greatest weakness — it lay at the point of his relationships. He always needed a sexual high to help him avoid the intimacy he feared. All his opponents had to do was bribe a beautiful Philistine woman named Delilah and suddenly, with his passions running wild, Samson was sleeping with the enemy.

These tragic stories in the Bible are not far removed from our day. Domestic violence and the AIDS epidemic have focused center-stage attention on the primacy of personal relationships. At age 33, basketball great "Magic" Johnson had an annual income of $17.5 million dollars a year, five world championship rings, a new wife, and a baby on the way. At age 46, football Hall of Famer O.J. Simpson had television and movie contracts and several million dollar properties. What more could a person want?

Samson, David, Bathsheba, "Magic" Johnson and O.J. Simpson have some things in common — they did not do drugs and they were not gay. They were just somewhat *naive* about the importance of human relationships. If there is a common thread from the ancient world to ours it is the fact that *those who are most at risk in terms of their health and their jobs are those who are naive about their relationships.*

One of the most penetrating novels you can read is *The Plague* by Albert Camus. The novel centers on a plague-ridden city in North Africa. A haunting vision of life comes forth when the narrator observes that there have been as many plagues as wars in history.[44] Yet plagues seem to catch us by surprise. We worry about wars and pray about conflicts. We light candles in churches for our relatives who are suddenly called up to go to the Persian Gulf. But no one lights a candle or calls me as university minister to express concern about Bob and Sally who are engaged in sexual behavior or drinking too much in one of the frat houses or their dorm room or apartment. I mean, why worry? They don't do drugs and they're not gay. We always find it hard to believe when the plagues of alcoholism, AIDS, and domestic violence crash down on our heads from a blue sky.

102

How are your relationships? Over 400,000 people have AIDS and over two million alcoholics *never* drank anything but beer. A soldier in combat in the Persian Gulf had a better chance of survival than two people *naive* about the importance of relationships.

Consider this. Here's Susan. She's an honors student. She has a 4.0 GPA at a major university. She's a class marshall. She's excelled in every course. She has been accepted to medical school. But Susan is lonely. She thinks sex is a way to become intimate. She's also one who closes off conversations when her angry feelings start to come out. She's a perfectionist. The thoughts of people not pulling their weight or a professor who would dare give her a *B* infuriate Susan.

Now, here's Betty. She was below the national average on all standardized tests but managed to throw together a 2.0 (*C* average) for four years. She's occasionally sloppy and will do things spontaneously. Her character is predictable. She sees other people as separate persons and doesn't try to merge with them or take them over.

Over the long haul of their lives, guess who will have a more successful career? Betty. Which one is most likely to have a happier marriage and a happier family? Betty. Which one is most likely to live longer? Betty.

Our success in the future will depend more on how we handle our relationships than it will on how we handle our property and our money.

In this respect I think we perhaps have misread Jesus' parable of the prodigal son. Isn't this really a parable indicting the father of the lost boy?

In Luke's fifteenth chapter the theme of the parable is loss. Jesus tells of three things that were lost. First he tells of a lost sheep. Then he tells of lost money. Finally he tells of a lost relationship.

In the case of the lost sheep, the shepherd went back over every step he had taken and searched in every ravine until he had regained the lost sheep. The woman who lost one of her coins swept every corner, looked under every bed, and fumbled behind every door until she had found her lost coin. But *nobody went out to look for this lost son.*[45]

Isn't that the way most humans react? The sheep was the shepherd's property. People will search high and low, long and hard, to regain lost property. Watch someone who has lost keys. Or witness the student who has lost a notebook. A huge poster goes up — "free beer from Kroger to the person who returns my jacket taken at homecoming." Our property is important. Everyone will rally around property. In fact, if you read most church histories and many brochures of universities, they are accounts of what building was built when. And we exonerate those people who, like the shepherd in the story, work long hours or give big gifts to help us acquire our property.

And, like the woman in the parable, most of us will work double shifts in order to regain lost money. Let me lose my wallet and I'll turn the house upside down trying to look behind every door and sweeping every corner looking for that lost money and those lost credit cards.

Ah, but Jesus nails us between the eyes in his final parable. Very few people bother themselves with trying to regain lost parents, lost sons, lost daughters, lost husbands, lost wives or even lost friends.

Wasn't there something just a little bit irritating about the father in this story of the prodigal son? He didn't hesitate to give his son all the property and money that he could. But when the boy was lost from himself, the father didn't go looking for him. Then, when the boy came to himself in the pigpen and returned home, the father ran down the road like a silly clown, killing the fatted calf, blowing money on a party, and inviting all the neighbors over.

Just might not Jesus have been trying to show us how silly we humans can be — doing anything within our power to go after lost property and lost money but sitting at home waiting on lost parents, lost sons, lost daughters, lost spouses, and lost friends to come to themselves?

It's strange what you and I will do to regain lost money and lost property but won't do to go after lost friends. But the key to life lies not in money and property but in relationships.

As the maps are redrawn for relationships, families, and social patterns in our pluralistic world, it will take a conscious effort to nurture a genuine interest in other people. The demands of the next century will call for genuine Christian ladies and gentlemen who can affirm the assets in other people. Timeless truths about human relationships will need to be revivified.

Men will need to realize that men were made to protect, love, and cherish women, not to undervalue, neglect, or abuse them. A gentlemen realizes that to degrade a woman is to degrade himself as a man. He realizes that her character is as sacred as his. Not to be like this is to fail in your relationships and fail as a person in our kind of world. Conversely, to be a woman and not expect a man to be a gentleman to you is to degrade yourself. If we are to emerge as sane and healthy people in the new century we will have to possess enough relational skills to distinguish authentic personhood from the counterfeit.

The Upward Pull

Have you ever wondered how some banks train people to detect counterfeit bills? Some fake money looks just like the real thing. The American Banking Association sponsors a two-week training program. The program is unique in how it helps tellers detect counterfeit bills. Not once during the two-week training does a teller ever see a single counterfeit bill. Not once do they listen to a lecture describing the characteristics of counterfeit money. All they do for two weeks is handle authentic currency. Hour after hour, and day after day they just handle the real stuff. *At the end of the training they have become so familiar with the authentic that they are never fooled by the false.*

Essentially, that's the Bible's approach to life. How, for example, does a great singer learn to detect bad or mediocre singing? Week by week, hour by hour, and day by day, he hones his craft. He sings the good stuff, associates with the best in his profession, tackles the tough notes, and strives to expand to his fullest capacity. At the end of the experience he has become so familiar with the good that he is never again fooled by the mediocre.

This perspective of the upward pull cuts against the grain of the common adage: "Well, I've got to see how the other half lives so I'll learn what not to be."

You know how this works: "Hey, I've got to try everything once so I'll know what to avoid. That's how you learn about right and wrong."

Not so. The law of the upward pull and the downward drift is a very big part of life.

One of my dearest friends in life was an elderly woman named Ruth Babb. She called me over to her home the very first week I was in the ministry. She gave me a piece of advice that I have found most helpful. She sat me down in an old rocking chair, looked me in the eye, and said, "Don't read what we read. We read *Reader's Digest, Time Magazine, Guideposts*, and Danielle Steele. Read better stuff than we read. Pull us up on Sunday morning. Lift us to a higher plane. Don't try to be popular. Pull me up."

The apostle Paul wrote some private letters to encourage two of his associates, Timothy and Titus. One theme is repeatedly emphasized in the correspondence. The theme is "godliness." The word "godliness" is only used fifteen times in the Bible and eleven of those occurrences are in these private letters. We are encouraged to train ourselves to be godly. We are urged to pursue *godliness*.

What in the world is *godliness*? Godliness is not just a warm, emotional feeling about God. It certainly gives us a warm feeling when we sing some grand old hymn like "Amazing Grace," but that isn't godliness. Private Bible study groups are very inspiring, but that alone isn't godliness.

Neither is godliness necessarily evidenced by conversations liberally seasoned with pietistic and heavenly sounding words like "the Lord" or "Jesus."

Actually, godliness seems to be a matter of focus, of looking up higher than yourself. Jesus once said,"If I be lifted up I will draw all people unto me." In like manner the Psalmist declared, "I will lift up my eyes to the hills." Apparently there is a law of the upward pull that operates in life.

I'm not a physicist or even a mathematician. But I do know this. You can take four apples and place one on each corner of a table. Tie a piece of string about three feet long to the stem of each apple. Gather the loose ends of the strings in your hand and raise your hand above the table until the strings become tight. As you tighten the strings by pulling upward the apples will all come together.

Essentially, says scripture, when men and women look upward, it's not just an individual phenomenon. All men and women are brought closer together in love and service when they lift up Christ.[46]

In short, surround yourself with people smarter than you are; align yourself with a cause that will outlive your own life. Otherwise, says Halford Luccock, "a college education may be merely the sharpening of claws for the competitive struggle so that one can get a bigger pile of loot."[47] A pile of loot is nice, but without an upward vision it can degenerate into an ingenious means of collective suicide.

Perhaps the twenty-first century will place more demands upon us for making critical life-and-death family and economic choices. Certainly we will have to live better with less. As the current generation gets caught in the squeeze between children who demand more goods and more costly education than past generations, and aging parents who consume more expensive medical resources for a longer period of time than ever before, the temptation to view solutions as sociological and/or governmental will be great. These horizontal problems, however, must be addressed by deep personal spirituality. As perhaps never before, Christians will be called to endorse their lives and release the power within themselves to live life afresh.

Chapter Five

Epilogue:
Endorsing The Future

One of the first things you do when you move to a new place is establish a checking account with a local bank. We can all tell stories of inexperienced people and their checking account problems. I remember a student who wrote check after check, only to discover he had no money left in his account. In exasperation he explained to the teller, "But I still have some checks left."

My sister-in-law, during her first semester in college, received a notice from the bank that she was $27.60 overdrawn in her account. She calmly sat down and mailed the bank a check for $27.60.

There was a young minister in graduate school who had never had a bank account. He was sent out to preach at a small country church. At the close of the service the treasurer gave him a check. He didn't know what to do with it. The treasurer told him if he would go to the bank the next morning before he left town that he could give it to the bank and they would give him cash for it. The next morning, feeling quite important, he went to the bank and handed the check to a teller. The teller turned it over and nothing happened because nothing was written on the back. She handed it back and said, "If you will just endorse this, I will be glad to cash it."

"Endorse it!" What's that? Well, he knew it had something to do with writing. He looked around and saw other people writing on the backs of checks. He spied a desk and a pen. After thinking for a few minutes, he signed his name. When he turned it in, the teller saw that he had written diagonally across the face of the check, "I heartily endorse the sentiments herein expressed. John R. Peterson."[48]

To endorse something is to attach your name publicly to a product, to throw your sentiments to an idea — to be committed. Unlike Eastern religions which focus on the revelation of God or the gods and goddesses in nature, the Western religions (Judaism, Christianity, and Islam) believe that God operates in history. Consequently, the Christian is called upon to endorse the time and place of his or her life as the arena of God's activity. Whatever God we encounter or confirm by our reason must be verified in our experience. If we are to live in the twenty-first century then we must endorse that world as the place of God's revelation. It will not do for us to create merely a safe haven for our own spirituality and cogitate on eternal, fixed truths. If feminist re-imagining of God, male movements, a re-ordered and more pluralistically composed religious landscape, and a more limited appraisal of American economic and political influence on the world is the reality of our history, then that is precisely where we must look for God's voice and God's activity. The acceptance of perceived limits is in reality a part of our Christian witness as well as our hope for a more meaningful future.

We all endorse certain sentiments that come our way in life. Some entertainers and coaches earn more from their endorsements than they do from practicing their professions.

One of the saddest stories of scripture to me is that of Joseph of Arimathea who came to claim Jesus' body. He was recorded as "a secret follower of Jesus." He wouldn't endorse Jesus in public but he followed him in private. He missed the essence of God's revelation to his world.

One day in Paris, Voltaire, who was generally regarded as an infidel (non-believer), was standing with a friend. A religious procession carrying a crucifix passed Voltaire. He lifted his hat as the crucifix passed. "What!" exclaimed the friend. "Are you reconciled to God?" With fine irony Voltaire replied, "We salute, but we do not speak."[49] In other words, it's nice, but don't count on me to endorse it publicly.

Some of the saddest stories in life have been those of great and talented people who, regardless of their accomplishments, just never endorsed the right thing. They never turned their lives totally over to the right power. They started out well and appeared to conquer the world. They lived life to the hilt, but then the betrayals and heartaches set in. Having never turned their lives over to Christ or any higher power, they eventually just quit on life since it did not resonate with any of their preconceived notions of what life should be like.

Such a man was found bruised and bleeding in a New York neighborhood. He was a common drunk. A passerby found him and took the drunk to Bellevue Hospital, where he died after three days. No one knew who he was. He had been admitted as John Doe. The filth, drugs, and loneliness that had been his lot were common among Bowery bums who drank themselves to death. A friend who had been looking for him for several weeks went to the city morgue and in desperation searched among the John Doe corpses. There he was, lying among the dozen other unidentified drunks. His friend gathered up all of John Doe's personal belongings: 38 cents and a scrap of paper that said "Dear friends and gentle hearts."

As it turned out, this drunk, whose life had led to despair and rage, actually had had the soul of a genius. Long before his tragic death at age 38, John Doe had written songs that have become deeply rooted in our southern heritage. John Doe had been known as Stephen Foster. He had written "Way Down Upon the Suwannee River," "Oh! Susanna," "Jeannie With the Light Brown Hair," "My Old Kentucky Home," and two hundred more wonderful songs like them. Then he gave up on life, having written so much about the past. Apparently, nostalgia for a culture long since past could not be replaced by a vision of God acting through present circumstances.

One thing we can be certain of — regardless of our talent, regardless of our education, regardless of our wealth —life at some point in the new century is going to test us. We will feel that we are *hopeless*. We are going to face some misery and considerable limits. And it doesn't matter whether we talk to the theologians or the psychiatrists, they will both tell us that people face limits in only one of three ways.

We can cry about our problems. We don't believe things will work out for us. We can languish in the tears of depression: "I knew it would be this way." We can stay in that desolate place and wallow down low, crying painful tears in the valley of our problems. We can literally cry over what we do not have. We can feel as if we are dead — we have a body, to be certain, but it's full of a dead person's bones. While others live up on the mountaintop of adventure, we can cry our tears in the valley of sorrow without working for change or insight. The elderly will be living longer and creating a host of bioethical dilemmas. The media will continue to exert a disproportionate influence on American values. Irresponsible sexuality will continue to flaunt itself in the face of the AIDS epidemic. We can languish in nostalgia, hoping for a return to the abnormal 1960s. We can even create our own little country club havens which resemble an old Kentucky home, Jeannie with the light brown hair, and way down upon the Suwannee River. After all, over 800 new "Christian" high schools were created in the past ten years and an abundance of candidates run for office who make us feel comfortable with our prejudices.

A second response to life's misery is to let it fester until it explodes in the anger of our self-centered cravings. We get hooked on our pessimism. We run into people who are narrow-minded and mean. We encounter prejudice and hate. We know that everyone is selfish, ruthless, and cruel. What can we expect from this crummy world, anyway? We better punch it in the nose before it punches us. Let's fight our way out of this valley of sorrow. We can take the offensive, yell reverse discrimination, close the borders to immigration, and turn on those we perceive to be the alien, the stranger, and the foreigner to our traditional cultural inheritance. And there is much support for this. The Western religions are exclusive religions and fundamentalism is worldwide. Countries ruled by dictators usually have the cleanest streets. We can employ "survival of our kind" techniques.

Gerald Kennedy tells the startling experience of a man who visited the Bell Laboratories. One of the executives had on his desk a machine that really represents the end of the line for many people. It was a small wooden casket the size of a cigar box. On its side was a single switch. Flip the switch and a hand emerges. The hand reaches down, turns off the switch and goes back into the box. When the lid comes down the buzzing stops. That's all there is to it — the machine does nothing but switch itself off.[50]

Obviously, it would seem funnier if it didn't symbolize so many human lives. There are people who wake each morning for no greater purpose than to pamper themselves, accumulate a few grown-up toys, and then switch themselves off again each evening. Then, when their battery, that old ticker called the heart, runs down, they can't even do that anymore. That's not much of a legacy to hand over to the twenty-second century.

Isaac Watts wrote a haunting poem. It went something like this:

> *There are a number of us creep*
> *Into this world, to eat and sleep;*
> *And know no reason why we're born,*
> *But only to consume the corn,*
> *Devour the cattle, fowl, and fish,*
> *And leave behind an empty dish.*
> . . . .
> *Then if their tombstone, when they die,*
> *(Doesn't) flatter and lie,*
> *There's nothing better will be said*
> *Than that "They've eat up all their bread,*
> *Drunk up their drink, and gone to bed."*

As I say, it's a haunting poem. We can indeed release all our energy eating our bread, drinking our drink, and going to bed. It's indeed possible to spend the energy of our lives loving only what we can use, worshipping only what we have bought, and believing only what we can see. And frankly, that's a waste, a tragic waste, because we never get all that energy and those years back in the future, even if we suddenly discover the twenty-first century is worth living in.

But there is, fortunately, a more Christian response to what life hands us at any moment within the world's history. We can surrender to one who is beyond the limited perception of our own history, endorse our lives and our times, and release the power of God which lies within the autobiography of our world.

Compared to our past American experience, white mainline Protestants may feel like strangers in Babylon in the twenty-first century. In terms of our heritage we will certainly be aliens in an unfamiliar place. Our traditional religious symbols and meanings could very well be removed from the land. We may be in exile, from the old ways, in our own country. Certainly we will no longer be the only dominant religious force shaping the American experience. As we become a minority, albeit the largest minority, in our own land we will face some of the same theological issues which faced those ancient Jews who woke up in Babylon. We will have to think through the double theme of relinquishing the old and receiving the new. The moral corruption of the clergy, the temptation toward formalism and legalism, and the appearance of the defeat of our former American way of life always call the presence of God into question. Are these other gods from the East stronger than Yahweh? Should we accommodate the New Age spirituality? Hadn't God promised us an eternal dynasty when those pilgrims sailed the ocean under the images of crossing the Red Sea into a new Israel?

While not in formal exile or slavery, we white Protestants will resemble a large ethnic group certainly cut off from its cultural surroundings. To many sitting here at the brink of the new century the ancient prophet Ezekiel and the voices of others who have found themselves in unfamiliar surroundings may be instructive.

The prophet Ezekiel was confronted in Babylon by God. He and his people were living in a dark valley. The valley was a symbol of their situation in Babylon. It was a low place. They were surrounded by economic mountains. Their jobs were gone. They were surrounded by social and political mountains — these teachers, scholars, philosophers, and leaders had hit rock bottom — prisoners of war. They were in a valley of sorrow. Some were crying and others were getting angry over their situation. They were figuratively dead people. They were aware of their limitations, their failures, their bleak future. They were in the valley of their trouble. Ezekiel saw wheels and he was carried up and around the valley so he could see every problem. And the question was put to him, "Can these people live?" You are a scientist, but can these people live? You are an educator, but can these people live? You are a psychologist who knows all about drives and reactions and responses and tendencies. With all this knowledge, can you answer me: "Can these people live?"

"Are they going to cry? Are they going to fight? Or are they going to endorse their lives over to me?"

Big question? So those Jews turned their lives over. Right there in that valley they just endorsed their lives over to the power of the universe. They let it loose and rose above their own time and place. Through their perceived darkness and tribulation, they just endorsed their lives over to God.

That message has been let loose time and time again when humans have found themselves in a perceived valley of sorrow.

In our own nation's past, a group of people arrived upon these shores of America, and to them it was a valley. To others it was a mountaintop of possibilities. To them it was a valley of slavery. They had no thought of ever having a chance to ride in one of the great chariots or surreys that they saw their bosses riding around in. Some cried and died. Some grew angry and festered and boiled inside. And some stood in the fields of North Carolina and Alabama and Mississippi and other places and said, "I will not live in this valley of sorrow. I refuse. One day a chariot is going to swing low enough for me." They sang: "Swing low, sweet chariot, coming for to carry *me* home."

Some cried tears of depression in that valley of sorrow: "I knew it would be this way." Others tried to fight and fester their way out of that valley. But others responded differently. They endorsed their lives, and moved beyond the tears and anger of defeat.

This is not a message from me. This is a message that was let loose by Ezekiel in Babylon 2,580 years ago. It was let loose again in the cotton fields of Mississippi 140 years ago. It wound its way to the coal fields of Appalachia and was let loose again just seventy years ago. It was bottled up in the blighted ghetto of Detroit and let loose again just twenty years ago. And it is lodged in your soul now. When life throws its worst at you, what will happen to you? Will you cry? Will you fight? Or will you endorse that power of God within you to believe in so much more than your smallness and let it loose? Can you make fresh, every day, the world around you and learn to renew life in the very crises and limitations which impinge upon you?

Fresh Every Day

How do we take the best we have inherited from our past and make it our own unique experience today? As we listen to stimulating patriotic music, explode firecrackers, head to the beaches, gather in our churches, or sit on the couch to view a ballgame on television, can you and I recover the intense awareness of living in a free country? This awareness obviously seemed very real, alive, and meaningful for Americans at various periods in our past.

Author William Gibson[51] describes an incident which took place in his life shortly after his mother died. Gibson was despondent. He did not seem to possess as strong a faith in God as he believed his mother to have possessed. God seemed so real, so alive, and so meaningful to her. But not to him. In desperation he decided to reach out for the slender thread of his mother's faith. He picked up his late mother's gold-rimmed spectacles and her faded, dog-eared prayer book. He went over to what was once his mother's favorite chair and sat in it. Very gently, he opened the book and tried to hear in those words what her ears must have heard. Then he placed her spectacles on his nose and tried to see what she must have seen in the prayer book. Gibson writes that he did not see what she had seen nor hear what she had heard.

It never works when we try to stoke the fires of another person's experience. We cannot live off a borrowed identity. Every generation has to reclaim its important beliefs, just as each individual has to carve out his or her own faith.

116

In this respect, as I search the scripture, I'm impressed by the urgency in the voices of angels.

The Bible reports that angels are always urgent when *they* talk to sleepyheads. They always say, "Arise. Get going, right now." An angel appears to Joseph in a dream, when Herod was slaughtering all those infants, and says, "Wake up. Go quickly." An angel appears to Philip in the Book of Acts and says, "Rise quickly." An angel says to Elijah, "Arise and eat." An angel comes to Peter in jail and says, "Rise quickly." The angels always say the same thing — "Hurry. Do it now." There's even an urgency in the voice of Jesus as He says to His disciples, "Follow me!"

The Bible has a persistent theme — great things have to be fresh. They have to be urgently gathered each time. The important things in life cannot be gathered in advance and embalmed, preserved or pickled. We cannot slouch our way toward any great belief.

When I was growing up, I had a next door neighbor named Pickle Keller. The Kellers were funny people. In a way, they were all somewhat pickled. They shopped for groceries once every three months. They would purchase a whole cow and stick it in their freezer and eat the meat until it was gone. My mother warned me never to eat lunch with the Kellers, for you never knew how old the meat was.

The Kellers never bought anything fresh. They went to a warehouse and purchased not a box, not a case, but a barrel of cereal. And once a year Pickle's mother would can things — fruits and vegetables. She'd put them on a shelf and they'd eat until they ran out. When it came to values and living, they lived a kind of pickled lifestyle, too. Ole Pickle's daddy was a patriot; everybody knew that. He'd fought in World War II: "The Big One," he called it. But he hadn't bothered to vote since he voted for Franklin Roosevelt. Nor was he ever involved in anything civic in the community. He'd secured that patriotism long ago. "Once a patriot, always a patriot," he said. At Christmas the Kellers went to church every time the door was opened — Sunday School, Sunday morning worship, Sunday evening worship, and Wednesday evening. They never came back until Easter. Then they'd show up again the Fourth of July. They worshipped in spurts. "Got enough religion when I was a boy to last me a lifetime," Pickle's daddy asserted. They subscribed to the adage, "train'em right when they're young and they'll grow in that direction."

The Book of Exodus contains an amazing story. It points to a truth far beyond the particulars of the historical event. The Israelites were complaining that they didn't have steady food like they'd had in Egypt. They were praying and fussing and complaining about their status on the journey to the promised land. "Give us meat," they beseeched. God gave them meat. Every evening quails came. Quails in that part of the world winter in Africa and migrate northward in the spring in vast flocks. This exhausting flight is done in stages. When the birds alight and take a rest in the evening, they are so tired they can easily be picked up by humans. God gave the Israelites quail.

But manna — now, that was something else. The Israelites also had to have bread. So God promised them bread in the mornings. The manna came on the tamarisk bushes. But there was a spiritual lesson in the manna. The manna comes from insects who eat the sap of the plant and pass the excess sap in honeydew excretions. The dry desert air changes those into drops that turn solid. But if you pick it and let it stay too long in the evening air, it spoils by the next morning.

As the people gathered this manna, they were warned by Moses not to gather more than enough for their family for one day. But some wanted security and collected enough for several days. The next morning they found the manna they had tried to store up had a foul odor and was full of worms.

The Bible is simply telling us that some things cannot be saved up for the future. Some values cannot be pickled or embalmed. They have to be constantly and urgently renewed. Jesus said the same thing when He taught us to pray, "Give us this day the bread for today." Some values have to be won every day, every time, every year. They are either freshly gathered or they become rotten.

Once we try to keep yesterday's sentiment for the future, it begins to smell. Look at patriotism, for example. Some people try to gather eloquent sentiments and embalm them. It's ridiculous to see someone wave the flag and scream "I'm for America" and then want to rest on his laurels. A patriot is someone who is doing something for America right now. A patriot is not someone who has some embalmed notions against the welfare state or creeping socialism but hasn't done one positive thing toward improving our country today — hasn't authored one constructive piece of legislation for America today. Just as soon as people no longer gather their civilization fresh each day, they tend to lose it. It spoils.

The church has to win its life every day or it will lose it. Its spirit has to be picked fresh with each generation or it begins to give off a foul odor. It does not matter how dedicated your charter members were to your church. It does not, from this perspective, matter how dedicated your parents were to Christ. Frankly, it may not matter how fervent was your conversion experience. Religion cannot be embalmed, saved up, or pickled. Jesus was right on the mark: "He who seeks to save his life will lose it." We have no Christian alternative but to endorse the world in which we live.

The problems of the twenty-first century are our opportunity, however great or small, to hear the voice of God as we regain a fresh sense of righteousness and justice.

Only when we stop shaming or inflating our time in which to live can we begin accepting ourselves and our God. We have memories and we have imaginations. There will always be a tension between what life was like in the past and what it could be like tomorrow. Those who cling to the past will ultimately cling to a corpse. God is the God of the living.

Perhaps we traditional Christians will never feel totally at home in the new century. We certainly will have to sacrifice some of our hard-won cultural gains in order to live within the new limits before us. We privileged white Protestants, Catholics, and Jews may have to be willing to die to self so that the good of all can prevail. We may have to give up our majority status so new religions can gain a foothold on our soil. We may need to sacrifice some of our prestige so other immigrants can have access to a free and meaningful public education. We may to sacrifice the old boy network so blacks, women, and others can have their moment in the sun. We may have to sacrifice our instant gratification so the

119

child of a single parent can enjoy benefits previously afforded only to the traditional family. A part of our life from the twentieth century may well have to die. Ultimately, all privileged people may have to die.

Carl Sagan and Ann Druyan are noted American scientists. They contend that however one understands the creation of the earth, there is one principle that made life possible and sustains it today. Without this principle, humans would never have come to be. They believe our earth had many creations and catastrophes, that life forms began and died out until this principle was enacted. There were many organic molecules that had the prospect of life, but these independent life forms died out. You see, there was no ozone to shield the surface of the earth from the searing ultraviolet light of the sun. The intensity of ultraviolet light at the surface of earth made it look like Mars today. The key to survival, with deadly ultraviolet light reaching the waters of earth, was *sunblock*. Stramatolite micro-organisms secrete a kind of extracellular glue that helps them stick together and adhere to the ocean floor. At an optimum depth in the ocean, not so shallow as to be fried by ultraviolet rays, and not so deep that too little light was available for photosynthesis, an amazing thing happened. The daughter cells of one-celled organisms did not separate and go their individual ways. Instead, they remained attached, and after many reproductions generated an irregular mass. If they had spread out thinly, all would have died. But clustered together the cells in the middle were shielded from the deadly radiation. Thus life was possible because of the principle of life itself: *some died that others might live.*[52]

That principle of life has made possible the transmission of genuine faith from generation to generation. It has enabled humankind to purify itself from the imperfections of society and to lift its soul toward the realm of God. This principle, for Christians, has been eternally embodied in the truth of the cross of Christ. In that truth, hopefully we citizens of the twenty-first century can liberate ourselves from the clutch of the past and create a better, more fully human future for a more pluralistic society. That liberation may, indeed, be our most decidedly Christian witness.

NOTES

1. As quoted by John Killinger in a sermon, "Living More In A World of Less," November 21, 1982.

2. Thanks to Will Willimon, "Unfinished Business," a 1991 Baccalaureate Sermon, Duke University. His telephone conversations were also most helpful.

3. Anna Quindlen, "Life in the 30's," *The New York Times*, June 9, 1988, p. C2.

4. Killinger, *op. cit.*, makes reference to this parable.

5. As reported by Gary C. Redding in "The First Word," Vol. 3, No. 32, North Augusta, S.C.

6. See the incisive book by Laurence Shamus, *The Hunger for More: Searching For Values In An Age of Greed* (New York: Times Books, 1989), especially pp. 28-35.

7. Nahum M. Sarna, General Editor, *The JPS Torah Commentary: Leviticus* (Philadelphia: The Jewish Publication Society, 1989), pp. 134-135. The Hebrew Text is that of the Leningrad Codex B 19a, the oldest dated manuscript of the complete Hebrew Bible.

8. Carlyle Marney, *Structures of Prejudice* (New York: Abingdon Press, 1961), p. 13. See pages 11-18 for an incisive commentary on human weakness and power.

9. Murdo Ewen Macdonald, *The Call to Obey* (London: Hodder and Stoughton, 1963), pp. 92-93, has an excellent commentary on Gandhi and Isaac Newton.

10. Richard Shenkman, *Legends, Lies, and Myths* (New York: William Morrow and Company, 1988), p. 84.

11. Winona Laduke, "We Are Still Here," *Sojourners* (October, 1991), p. 12.

12. Harold Cooke Phillips, "Closing the Door," in *Sunday Evening Sermons*, ed. by Alton M. Motter (New York: Harper), p. 91.

13. *Hazelden Meditations*, June 15, 1986.

14. As used by Charles L. Allen in *The Miracle of Hope* (Old Tappan, N.J.: Fleming H. Revell Co., 1983), pp. 16-17.

15. See John Howard Yoder, *The Politics of Jesus* (Grand Rapids, Mich.: Wm. B. Eerdmans, 1972), p. 61.

16. Ernest A. Fitzgerald, *How To Be A Successful Failure* (New York: Athenaeum, 1978), pp. 6-8.

17. As told by Bruce McLeon, *City Sermons* (Burlington, Ontario, Canada: Welch Publishing Company, 1986), pp. 69-71.

18. Jimmy Buffett, "Fruitcakes." 1994 Coral Reefer Music (BMI)/Publick Ptomaine Music (BMI).

19. F.F. Bruce, *The Hard Sayings of Jesus* (Downers Grove, Ill.: Inter Varsity, 1983), pp. 94-95.

20. Carlyle Marney, "Our Present Higher Good," in *To God Be The Glory*, ed. by Theodore Gill (Nashville: Abingdon, 1973), pp. 52-61.

21. Tom Downing, "The Great Ascent," a sermon preached October 20, 1985.

22. Murdo E. Macdonald, *The Call to Obey*, (London: Hodder & Stoughton, 1963), p. 24. This book is an excellent resource, especially the chapter "Is Morality Enough?"

23. Thanks to Harold G. Newsham, *The Man Who Feared A Bargain* (New York: Abingdon), p. 45.

24. See Helmut Thielicke, *The Waiting Father* (New York: Harper & Row), translated by John W. Doberstein.

25. Shaw, as cited in K. Morgan Edwards, *Hoping To Be Somebody* (New York: Abingdon Press, 1959), pp. 88-89.

26. *Hazelden Meditations*, June 18, 1992 (Harper & Row).

27. Helmut Thielicke, *op. cit.*, pp. 45-47.

28. Gary C. Redding, "The First Word," N. Augusta, S.C., Vol. 3, No. 39, 17 Nov. 1991, p. 3.

29. Patricia Volk, "Being Safe," *New York Times*, 11 February 1990.

30. Carlyle Marney, *The Coming Faith* (Nashville: Abingdon, 1970), p. 157.

31. Herbert O'Driscoll, *Prayers for the Breaking of Bread* (Cambridge, Mass.: Cowley Publications, 1991), p. 10.

32. Donald R. Nichols, "The Myth of Corporate Excellence," delivered at the National Association for Corporate Speaker Activities, Oklahoma City National Conference, September 27, 1985.

33. Thomas J. Peters and Robert H. Watterman, Jr. *In Search of Excellence* (New York: Harper & Row, 1982), p. 37.

34. See Ella Pearson Mitchel, ed., *Those Preachin' Women* (Valley Forge: Judson, 1985), especially Carolyn Ann Knight, "The Survival of the Unfit," pp. 27-33.

    *See also, Helmut Thielicke, *The Great Adventure* (Philadelphia: Fortress, 1985), for an excellent analysis of Luke 7:36-50, especially pp. 72-78. Another good analysis of the same pericope is Robert Escamilla, *A Feast of Life* (Nashville: Tidings, 1972), pp. 41-45.

35. William J. Bennett, "The Index of Leading Cultural Indicators," Vol. I, 1993, p. ii.

36. National Center for Health Services.

37. David T. Ellwood, *Poor Support: Poverty in the American Family* (New York: Basic Books, 1988).

38. Leo Madow, *Anger: How to Recognize and Cope with It* (New York: Charles Scribner & Sons, 1972), p. 20.

39. *Ibid.*, p. 29.

40. Frederick Buechner, *Telling Secrets* (San Francisco: Harper, 1991) p. 10.

41. See Sam Keen, *Fire In the Belly* (New York: Bantam, 1991), p. 103.

123

42. See *His Hands: Resources for Lent and Easter*, ed. John Levinson (Lima, Ohio: CSS Publishing, 1977), p. 64.

43. Doris Donnelly, *Learning to Forgive* (New York: Macmillan, 1979), pp. 24-25.

44. Albert Camus, *The Plague*, Modern Library Edition, p. 34.

45. C.L. Franklin provides this insight into the Prodigal Son, in C.L. Franklin, *Give Me This Mountain*, ed. by Jeff Todd Titon (University of Illinois Press, 1989), pp. 56-57.

46. Clyde Foushee, *Animated Object Talks* (Fleming H. Revell, 1956), p. 13.

47. Robert E. Luccock, ed., *Halford Luccock Treasury* (New York: Abingdon, 1963), p. 113.

48. As told by Earl V. Pierce in *The Supreme Beatitude* (New York: Fleming H. Revell Company, 1947), p. 23.

49. Ben Lacy Rose, *On Your Way Rejoicing* (New York: Carlton Press Inc., 1991), p. 83.

50. Gerald Kennedy, *The Parables* (New York: Harper and Brothers, 1960), p. 38.

51. See Roger Lovette, *A Faith of Our Own* (Philadelphia: United Church Press, 1976), p. 129.

52. Carl Sagan and Ann Druyan, *Shadows of Forgotten Ancestors* (New York: Random House, 1992), p. 26.

www.ingramcontent.com/pod-product-compliance
Lightning Source LLC
LaVergne TN
LVHW022317080426
835509LV00036B/2570